GUEST-EDITED BY
BOB SHEIL

HIGH DEFINITION
ZERO TOLERANCE IN DESIGN AND PRODUCTION

01 / 2014

ARCHITECTURAL DESIGN
JANUARY/FEBRUARY 2014
ISSN 0003-8504

PROFILE NO 227
ISBN 978-1118-451854

AD

ARCHITECTURAL DESIGN

GUEST-EDITED BY
BOB SHEIL

HIGH DEFINITION: ZERO TOLERANCE IN DESIGN AND PRODUCTION

54

3D scanning provides entirely new avenues of understanding and engagement with the complexities of context, form, behaviour and volume that heretofore have been unattainable, crudely approximated or poorly grasped ... 'zero tolerance' is presented as a strategic choice to negotiate, rather than a narrow goal to aim for.
— Bob Sheil

82

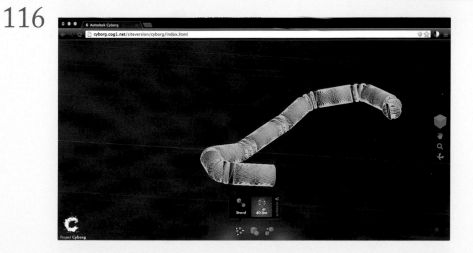

116

100748183x

Editorial Offices
John Wiley & Sons
25 John Street
London WC1N 2BS
UK

T: +44 (0)20 8326 3800

Editor
Helen Castle

Managing Editor (Freelance)
Caroline Ellerby

Production Editor
Elizabeth Gongde

Prepress
Artmedia, London

Art Direction and Design
CHK Design:
Christian Küsters
Sophie Troppmair

Printed in Italy by Printer Trento Srl

Subscribe to AD

AD is published bimonthly and is
available to purchase on both a
subscription basis and as individual
volumes at the following prices.

Prices
Individual copies: £24.99 / US$45
Individual issues on *AD* App
for iPad: £9.99 / US$13.99
Mailing fees for print may apply

Annual Subscription Rates
Student: £75 / US$117 print only
Personal: £120 / US$189 print and
iPad access
Institutional: £212 / US$398 print
or online
Institutional: £244 / US$457
combined print and online
6-issue subscription on *AD* App
for iPad: £44.99 / US$64.99

Subscription Offices UK
John Wiley & Sons Ltd
Journals Administration Department
1 Oldlands Way, Bognor Regis
West Sussex, PO22 9SA, UK
T: +44 (0)1243 843 272
F: +44 (0)1243 843 232
E: cs-journals@wiley.com

Print ISSN: 0003-8504
Online ISSN: 1554-2769

Prices are for six issues and include
postage and handling charges.
Individual-rate subscriptions must be
paid by personal cheque or credit card.
Individual-rate subscriptions may not
be resold or used as library copies.

All prices are subject to change
without notice.

Rights and Permissions
Requests to the Publisher should be
addressed to:
Permissions Department
John Wiley & Sons Ltd
The Atrium
Southern Gate
Chichester
West Sussex PO19 8SQ
UK

F: +44 (0)1243 770 620
E: permreq@wiley.com

FSC MIX
Paper from
responsible sources
FSC® C015829
www.fsc.org

Front cover: ScanLAB Projects, Terrestrial laser
scan of rock formations in Joshua Tree National
Park, California, part of the LA Skin Deep series,
2012. © ScanLAB Projects Ltd

Inside front cover: Territorial Agency, Multi-year
spectral analysis, Athabasca oil sands, Alberta,
Canada, 2013. © Territorial Agency 2013.
Landsat data elaborated with David Hellström

EDITORIAL
Helen Castle

△'s impulse is always towards the pioneering – its natural proclivity is to look forwards, anticipating just how fecund new developments in technology might prove to architecture. As Professor of Architecture and Design through Production and Director of Technology at the Bartlett School of Architecture, University College London (UCL), Bob Sheil has established a considerable reputation for a deep and sustained interest in fabrication attested by his previous publications for *△* and the seminal 'Fabricate' conference that he co-founded with Ruairi Glynn.[1] This issue's focus on verification technologies, specifically 3D scanning and its associated interface with modelling and manufacture, represents a significant shift. It also, as Sheil states in his introduction, gives us the sense of an 'air of a new frontier opening up' (pp 8–19).

The issue delivers much that is exciting at the cutting edge of technology with Tobias Nolte and Andrew Witt's description of the self-optimisation system that Gehry Technologies developed for the realisation of the Fondation Louis Vuitton art museum in Paris (pp 82–9). Skylar Tibbits also provides an insightful account of the 4D printing processes that the Self-Assembly Lab at the Massachusetts Institute of Technology (MIT) is collaborating on with multi-material printing company Stratasys Ltd (pp 116–121). New developments in technology often highlight or accentuate existing possibilities and preoccupations in design. This is an important aspect that Sheil gives space to in the issue by dedicating several articles to defining a high-definition approach and the perceptions surrounding it, whether informed by innovative or conventional techniques – see Ilona Gaynor and Benedict Singleton (pp 48–53), Birgir Örn Jónsson (pp 54–9) and Michael Webb's (pp 60–73) articles.

With new technologies, existing fissures within and between disciplines are often in danger of becoming drawn further apart. This issue focuses on the meaning of tolerance across conditions of fine-grain information, predominantly from a design perspective, but there is also the sense that we need to remain attentive of the opportunities that might be afforded, or lost, across practice and within the construction industry. Ruairi Glynn (pp 100–05) warns that the clunky and cumbersome nature of practice might prove a hurdle too far for the widespread adoption of hyper-connective, high-definition sensing among the profession, despite being wholeheartedly embraced by students in architecture schools. In a poignant Counterpoint to the issue (pp 128–32), Branko Kolarevic reminds us of the attitude of the building industry and the 'messy' realities of the construction site that design parameters are imported into. *△*

Note
1. Bob Sheil is the guest-editor of *△ Design Through Making*, July/August (no 4), 2005 and *△ Protoarchitecture: Analogue and Digital Hybrids*, July/August (no 4), 2008; and the editor of *Manufacturing the Bespoke: Making and Prototyping Architecture*, *△* Reader, Wiley (Chichester), 2012. The founding 'Fabricate' conference (15–16 April 2011) was co-chaired at the Bartlett School of Architecture, UCL, by Bob Sheil and Ruairi Glynn.

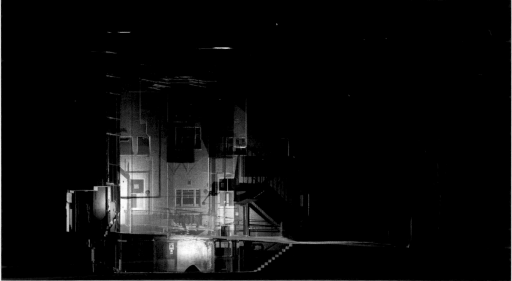

Protoarchitecture Lab, The Perform Project at the Royal Central School of Speech and Drama, University of London, 2013

top: Point cloud model of tests for the Perform project that involved robotic arms, moving reflecting surfaces and 3D scanning.

bottom: Point cloud model of the western elevation of the Royal Central School of Speech and Drama. The model captures one of three spaces in or around the building that hosted a series of collaborative experiments in architecture, scenography, performance and 3D scanning in September 2013.

Bob Sheil is an educator, researcher, practitioner, designer, maker and writer whose work is focused on the transgression between making, craft, digital fabrication, design processes and the impact of evolving design technologies on architecture. He is an international speaker and critic, a collaborator on built works, publications, events and projects, and has recently set up and directs the Protoarchitecture Lab at University College London (UCL). He is Professor in Architecture and Design through Production and Director of Technology at the Bartlett School of Architecture, UCL, where he also runs MArch Unit 23 with Emmanuel Vercruysse and Kate Davies of Liquidfactory. He is also a founding partner of sixteen*(makers), whose design for an experimental building (55/02) in collaboration with Stahlbogen GmbH won a RIBA award for design in 2010. He has guest-edited two previous issues of △: *Design Through Making* (July/Aug 2005) and *Protoarchitecture: Analogue and Digital Hybrids* (July/Aug 2008), as well as the △ Reader *Manufacturing the Bespoke: Making and Prototyping Architecture* (2012).

Sheil has also been published in several international peer-reviewed journals, including *Architectural Research Quarterly*, *The Journal of Architecture*, *Space* and *Nexus*, and has presented key papers, lectures and talks in the US, China and Europe. In 2011 he co-founded and co-chaired, with Ruairi Glynn, the highly acclaimed international 'Fabricate' conference at the Bartlett, UCL, for which he also co-edited a substantial parallel publication. He is an advisor to the second 'Fabricate' conference to be held at ETH Zurich in February 2014. In 2012 he edited *55/02: A sixteen*(makers) Project Monograph* (Riverside Architectural Press); he is currently working on a collaborative design project with the Royal Central School of Speech and Drama, the artists' collective Shunt, and ScanLAB Projects.

High Definition: Zero Tolerance in Design and Production defines a shift in the emphasis of his past publications that have covered the subjects of design and making in the digital age, particularly around the role of the designer as a maker. In this instance, he is drawing our attention to verification technologies, particularly 3D scanning and its associated interface with modelling and manufacture. The 21st century has begun with an explosion of new tools, techniques and methods, as well as a mounting catalogue of challenges facing the designer. Rather than be expected to master any one tool or set of tools, future designers must balance the role of evaluator and end-user programmer as they reinforce their role as visionaries in a dense cloud of information and expectations. As the potential to develop ever more precise data increases, this collection of diverse essays seeks to define a critical position in relation to the habit of continuously pushing limits. △

HIGH DEFINIT

NEGOTIATING ZERO
TOLERANCE

Tom Svilans, The Bradbury Transcripts, Unit 23, Bartlett School of Architecture, University College London (UCL), 2012–13
The fragmentation of the Bradbury Building into an 'architecturalised film sequence' seeks to address the continuity between actual and implied space, and the slippery territory between fact and constructed fiction. The image illustrates a panoramic of the 'studio' setup.

The limits of photography cannot yet be predicted. Everything to do with it is still so new that even initial exploration may yield strikingly creative results. Technical expertise is obviously the tool of the pioneer in this field. The illiterates of the future will be the people who know nothing of photography rather than those who are ignorant of the art of writing.

—Walter Benjamin (1928)[1]

Over the course of the last decade, the focal point for advanced technologies in architectural design has shifted from the outer edges of the virtual to a position of hybridity with the actual. The tangible has caught up with the intangible, and possibilities that were entirely speculative in non-physical domains just a few years ago are now being materialised and built. The term 'digital' no longer only conjures up notions of complex representation, computational geometries and intelligent systems, but also fabrication, craft and materials. At the same time, designers are faced with (and connected to) more tools to make their work than ever before, each packing extraordinary power, accuracy, capability and provocation. Subsequently, the scope on how these tools influence, validate or facilitate the designer is expanding rapidly and the challenge is to navigate such dynamic circumstances with a clear sense of critique on how they assist in advancing architecture as a visionary practice and subject.

Michelangelo Merisi da Caravaggio, *The Incredulity of Saint Thomas*, 1601–02
'Unless I see the nail marks in his hands and put my finger where the nails were, and put my hand into his side, I will not believe it.'
John 20:24.

More recently the tool range has taken an abrupt leap forward in the realm of definition and accuracy, and this issue of Δ is positioned as a critical reflection on what this means. It gathers an international and diverse collective of inquisitive and critical innovators whose work is exploring uncharted territory with measured curiosity. It speculates on how we might operate in the near future with inspiring and sobering insight, and presents a series of challenging questions that address designers' values in relation to the production of their work. Underlying the issue is the core relationship between digital technology and the designer's intent, where the meaning of tolerance is explored across conditions of fine-grain information, the management of complex processes, and engaging with the difference between the simulated and the built.

The Digital Generation

The typical undergraduate entering an architecture course today was six years of age at the turn of the millennium. They were born in the same year as the Apple QuickTake, the first commercially available digital camera. They took their first steps as the World Wide Web entered our homes, and built-in satellite navigation systems were available in production automobiles. By the time our present freshers were 10 years of age, Facebook was launched and Concorde had made its last commercial flight. In their teens, perhaps the time when they first contemplated reading architecture, the digitalisation of the Information Age was in full flow, 3D printing was mainstream, and both the construction and design industries were exchanging protocols on manufacturing processes. By the time they were accessing their first university podcast lecture, they were simultaneously downloading a plug-in upgrade and uploading their own latest applet development. Students today, and the architects of tomorrow, are the first generation entirely raised in a digital culture. They have been shaped by a period of profound and dynamic change, and they are entirely familiar with technologies that are always new. In this context, this issue of Δ also attempts to navigate a critical path through present evolutions that are occurring so thick and fast that the cloud we should be most concerned about is the one that obscures vision, on all sides.

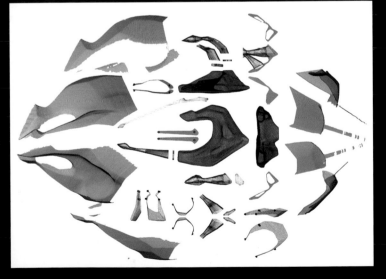

Matthew Shaw, Subverted Lidar Landscape, London, Unit 23, Bartlett School of Architecture, University College London (UCL), 2008–09
The zone of ambiguity. Point cloud model of the territory surrounding London's Houses of Parliament developed from aerial-captured lidar data. The location and its manipulated lidar portrait became the site for a speculative project investigating scanning technology, material behaviour, and laws for public gathering.

A series of prototypical objects explore the form and materiality of stealth and subversion. Each object starts life as an intuitively carved wooden sketch. These become 3D notebooks on which to design precise insertions and additions. The objects are then 3D scanned using a self-built scanner to enable precision inserts to be machined and added to the originals. These objects are then scanned and their digital siblings cast and machined from the scanned data.

Acts of Deception

Reality in the 21st century is increasingly defined by the untrustworthiness of its representation. Seeing is deceiving. Whether for artistic, commercial or political ends, images mediate our understanding of the world, conjuring powerfully convincing secondary narratives that can serve to reveal truth, obscure it or reinvent it entirely. Reality is constructed from what we are given to believe and all, it seems, is not as it seems.
— Kate Davies, Co-tutor, Unit 23, Bartlett School of Architecture, UCL, 2012[2]

55/02 is an experimental building by sixteen*(makers) and Stahlbogen GmbH, and was completed in 2009 at the steel fabricator's factory in Blankenburg, Germany.[3] The story behind this project and accounts on its design and hybridised digital production are documented elsewhere.[4] However, the images here talk of reflective observations made a year and more beyond its assembly on site at Kielder Water and Forest Park, Northumberland, UK, and are produced through 3D lidar scanning, executed by ScanLAB Projects, between March and June 2010.

One image presents an overlay of the 3D scan upon the digital design model. In other words, the 'built-record' model superimposed upon the 'design-record' model, where difference is clearly measurable.[5] Given the approach and experimental design and fabrication tactics of the project, differences were actively encouraged and entirely expected, yet their specifics were not known prior to such mapping. Although in this instance such difference is not of any critical status, the exercise revealed the persistence of translation issues between the drawn and the made, even in the digital age.

In an age of increasingly vertiginous standards in visual definition, boundaries between the real and the digital are becoming imperceptible and our visual literacy is fundamentally challenged and infused with suspicion and doubt. As Kate Davies says, 'Seeing is deceiving', and the tactile experience of engaging with the physical properties of design has therefore become an act of verification upon the visceral and cerebral construct. In this regard, the inclusion of exquisite new work by the visionary architect Michael Webb (pp 60–73), and the seemingly polar opposite world of the Centre for Advanced Spatial Analysis (CASA) at the Bartlett School of Architecture, University College London (UCL) (pp 40–47), is a deliberate move to frame the arguments of this issue in the broadest of terms. For the former, the meticulous layering and accretion of material and meaning upon a long and extended conversation of time, space, motion, geometry and fabrication talks of high definition as a theoretical assemblage of spatialised imaginings. For the latter, the theme is addressed as a revelation on the saturation of urban geographies through subliminal and parasitical technologies for which the city's inhabitants are both prey and predator.

sixteen*(makers) and Stahlbogen GmbH, 55/02, Kielder Water and Forest Park, Northumberland, UK, 2009
NW PROJECTION: Kielder 07.03.10 1643hrs. Section through a point cloud model from a lidar scan of the 55/02 shelter using a FARO Photon 120. Captured one year post-completion, the part re-representation was the guest-editor's first engagement with scanning technology, made available through an equipment load to University College London (UCL).

High Definition

High Definition: Zero Tolerance in Design and Production is the fourth ∆ publication of a sequence spanning the past decade that attempt to fathom technological evolutions through the discipline of making things.[6] As the array of tools to propose and make ideas has become significantly enriched in recent decades, the component of armoury that has remained out of step with potential has been the means to navigate, embed and verify design outcomes as they emerge in context.[7] Without such tools, the advancing of greater levels of precision, complexity and composition through design representation and production is unmatched by resources in execution and delivery. This issue extends the publication sequence by exploring ideas surrounding the alignment of the virtual and the real, and adopts as its springing point the 'new' discipline of 3D scanning, also known as light detection and ranging technology (lidar).[8]

With its roots in the automotive production industry, and applications in crime forensics, mining and marine engineering, mechanical verification, medicine and landscape, 3D scanning provides entirely new avenues of understanding and engagement with the complexities of context, form, behaviour and volume that heretofore have been unattainable, crudely approximated or poorly grasped. While specifications will be upgraded within months of this publication's release, the ability of today's instruments to measure beyond 150 metres (492 feet) at speeds up to 976,000 points per second with an error of +/− 2 millimetres (0.08 inches) breaches a significant tipping point on the status and utility of three-dimensional data capture.

Like all new assets in the visionary's toolbox, there is the air of a new frontier opening up as a result of these changes. However, as this collection of essays seeks to portray, it is a frontier where the same tools may be deployed to liberate or constrain, to facilitate or obstruct. For with high levels of precision comes scrutiny, and with that an expectation that difference between representation and the represented can be eliminated or glossed over. In so doing, we are in danger of producing 'botox' architecture that displays no trace of the decisions and actions that informed its production through the many tacit experiences that cannot be drawn, specified or defined in text, or indeed strategies that allow for the impact of a design's own life experience as an artefact residing in a messy world. In this regard, 'zero tolerance' is presented as a strategic choice to negotiate, rather than a narrow goal to aim for.

Negotiating Zero Tolerance

In the pages ahead, and occupying a central position among a high-calibre and distinguished group of contributors, the emerging portfolio of young practitioners and budding academics ScanLAB Projects illustrates an extraordinary range of experimental executions dispersed across distant geographic poles and exquisitely intimate scales (pp 20–29). Their inquisitive and intelligent voyage away from mainstream practice into new territories of spatial and material understanding is defining new roles and opportunities for the designer as an activist and inter-disciplinary collaborator, and their contribution is a cornerstone to the publication. Explorations, projects and critique on high-definition technologies are extended by the equally fascinating studies on remote urban settlements by Territorial Agency (pp 30–39), on peripheral vision by Birgir Örn Jónsson (pp 54–9), ideas of 'aesthetic precision' in architecture and cinema by Ilona Gaynor and Benedict Singleton of The Department of No (pp 48–53), and an exciting new collaboration between the architect/ craftsman Philip Beesley and the film director/cinematographer Philippe Baylaucq (pp 90–99).

Alignment of the made and the drawn. 55/02 was designed as an evolving physical and digital prototype where its CAD data was deployed as a manufacturing and feedback tool, as well as a digital record of analogue decisions made on the shop floor. The image illustrates an overlay of the 3D lidar scan upon the final production model. Where the image is red, the alignment matches; where it veers to grey and white it misaligns.

Tom Smith, Simulating a Crashed Architecture, Unit 23, Bartlett School of Architecture, University College London (UCL), 2011–12

top: Simulating a Crashed Architecture, alternative view. The project raises challenging questions on the seductive qualities of high-definition unreal architectural visualisations. The key to Smith's skilful draughtsmanship is to manage the balance between complex dynamic modelling and his deliberate cartoon-esque aesthetics.

Madhav Kidao, The Theatre of Synthetic Realities, Unit 23, Bartlett School of Architecture, University College London (UCL), 2011–12

opposite: A series of real and fictitious locations and events, actors and devices that attempt to question our production, embodiment and perception of social space as mediated through technology. The project examines how *The Internet of Things* extends beyond objects to Architecture and space, actions and interactions, forming a global digital record of physical memories.

bottom: Questioning the role of the architect, both in regard to creative authorship and ethical responsibility, semi-guided machines construct their own reality based upon the information they extract from their environment and its unwilling occupants.

From the field of industry in collaboration with academe, Tobias Nolte and Andrew Witt on Gehry Partners' Fondation Louis Vuitton (pp 82–9), through the lens of Gehry Technologies, is a fascinating analysis on how flows of highly complex design information and design production processes are meshing in the delivery of building forms not conceivable without bespoke tools. On a far smaller scale, but no less fascinating and pioneering, from the field of manufactured and behavioural hybrids are a series of short essays on new works by a generation of highly talented designer/tutors: Ruairi Glynn (pp 100–105), Marta Malé-Alemany and Jordi Portell (pp 122–7), and Brandon Kruysman and Jonathan Proto of Kruysman-Proto (pp 106–11). This work is included as key evidence of the vital and fluid relationship between a handful of key design studios in London, Europe and California that are each engaged with new and raw questions on how emerging forms of design production and development identify new ideas for architecture as an action of continuous prototyping.

Concurrent to the overview of work involving detection technology, this issue of ⊿ also draws into focus some new developments in the arena of production technologies, particularly in regard to definition and accuracy at medium to small scales. Here, operating in the context of nano-manufacturing, are Skylar Tibbits's innovations in 4D manufacturing (pp 116–21), an avenue of research that transforms preconceived notions of assembly and use. See also the latest work from Richard Beckett and Sarat Babu of the Bartlett's Manufacturing and Design Exchange (BMADE) (pp 112–15), who are testing polymer printing technologies to their physical and material limits, and thereby continually challenging the status of the work between design verification tooling and high-precision batch manufacturing. And finally in this category, we get behind the scenes of a new work by the artist Richard Wilson through an account by engineers Ralph Parker and Tim Lucas (pp 74–81), whose discipline it is to make the illusion.

Fabricating the Real

Alongside colleagues Kate Davies and Emmanuel Vercruysse, MArch Unit 23 at the Bartlett School of Architecture, UCL is led as a critical research environment associated with the school's extensive workshop facilities in CAD/CAM, 3D manufacturing, 3D scanning and robotics, where all are seen and used as agents provocateurs for both the representation and making of architectural speculation. Prompted by these and other emerging technologies, the unit's trajectory of annual thematic focus[9] is allied to evolving questions on the designer's role and expertise.[10] The student work featured in this Introduction traces the unit's history of experimentation that has led to this publication. For example, Matthew Shaw's earliest investigations into 3D scanning and its disruption of prior understandings between the drawn, the made, the built and the measured. His thesis 'Subverting the Lidar Landscape' (2007–08) established a very clear platform for the founding of ScanLAB Projects along with fellow Unit 23 graduate William Trossell. Their pioneering work forms the backbone of this ⊿.

Tom Smith, Simulating a Crashed Architecture, Unit 23, Bartlett School of Architecture, University College London (UCL), 2011–12
Drawing on JG Ballard's fascination with the 'crashworthiness' of a car, this project is a richly saturated orgy of precision inspired by both the meticulous reconstructions of crash-test simulation rigs and highly articulated animations that replay a precisely choreographed sequence of high-speed architectural collisions in luxurious slow motion.

Moving ahead to 2011–12 is the fascinating work of Madhav Kidao and his curious and knowing navigation of 'saturated space', the contemporary experience of living in a sea of data flow. Of the same vintage, both Tom Smith and Joseph Ransom Shaw (2011–12) convey a sense of recalibrating the real through the lens of high-definition digital animation. In both instances, the authors are commenting on the 21st-century dependency and subsequent addiction to the unreal, the unmade, the hyper-real and the immersive environments of digital simulation.

Finally, incorporating the scripted choreography of a high-definition digital camera on a programmed robotic arm that sweeps through a series of physical and digital spatialised models, Tom Svilans's project The Bradbury Transcripts (2012–13), based within the Bradbury Building in Los Angeles (the site of many movie and television shoots), takes the question of where the architecture is being made a step further. Tapping into the building's mythology as a filmic site and host to technological fictions, 'real' contexts are meshed with fictional histories through seamless and ambiguous representations.

On this note, *High Definition: Zero Tolerance in Design and Production* is presented as an array of speculative and diverse essays, each defining an argument on how our discipline tackles and manages the relentless momentum that empowers the technologies of representation and making to compulsive degrees of simulated accuracy. Perhaps the question to ask is not how difference between design and production can be eliminated, but how it can be valued? ∆

Notes
1. Cited in David Mellor (ed), *Germany: The New Photography 1927–33*, Arts Council of Great Britain (London), 1978, p 20.
2. Kate Davies, 'Acts of Deception', Unit 23, Bartlett School of Architecture, University College London (UCL), 2012–13 programme, with Bob Sheil and Emmanuel Vercruysse: see http://tinyurl.com/pm4n3w3.
3. Bob Sheil (ed), *55/02: A sixteen*(makers) Project Monograph*, Riverside Architectural Press (Toronto), 2012.
4. For example, see Neil Spiller, 'The Mathematics of the Ideal Pavilion', in Nic Clear (ed), ∆ *Architectures of the Near Future*, Vol 79, No 5, Sept/Oct, 2009, pp 124–5.
5. Bob Sheil, 'De-Fabricating Protoarchitecture', *Prototyping Architecture: The Conference Papers*, Building Centre Trust (London), 2013, pp 372–90: www.buildingcentre.co.uk/Prototyping%20 Architecture.pdf.
6. See also Bob Sheil (ed), ∆ *Design Through Making* Vol 75, No 4, July/Aug 2005; ∆ *Protoarchitecture: Analogue and Digital Hybrids*, Vol 78, No 4, July/Aug, 2008; and *Manufacturing the Bespoke: An ∆ Reader*, John Wiley & Sons (London), 2012.
7. Bob Sheil, 'De-Fabricating Protoarchitecture', op cit.
8. Emitting upwards of 100,000 pulses per second, lidar technology involves a scanning and ranging laser system that produces pinpoint-accurate, high-resolution topographic maps. The original technology has been in existence for 20 to 30 years, but the commercial applications for lidar-generated topographic maps have only developed within the last decade. Today the entire process of airborne laser mapping is highly automated, from flight planning to data acquisition, to the generation of digital terrain models. The basic components of a lidar system are a laser scanner and cooling system, a global positioning system (GPS), and an inertial navigation system (INS). Information obtained from Airborne 1 (http://airborne1.com/). See also the US Geological Survey (USGS) Center for Lidar Information Coordination and Knowledge: http://lidar.cr.usgs.gov/.
9. Unit 23 themes have reflected an interest in setting new agendas for architecture as new design and fabrication technologies have emerged in the last decade: Transplants/Transactions (2003–4); Made in London (2004–5); Codemaker (2005–6); Transgression (2006–7); Protoarchitecture (2007–8); Manufacturing the Bespoke (2008–9); (extra) ordinary (2009–10); The Laboratory of Experimental Fabrication and Technology (2010–11); Fabricating the Real (2001–12); Acts of Deception (2012–13). See http://www.bartlett.ucl.ac.uk/architecture.
10. Adjacent workshop and laboratory facilities are now grouped under the school's new organisational structure for design production known as the Bartlett Manufacturing and Design Exchange (B>MADE).

Joseph Ransom Shaw, The Unnatural History Unit, Unit 23, Bartlett School of Architecture, University College London (UCL), 2011–12
A polemical enquiry into the authenticity of TV documentaries as a sequence of spectacular studio-sets carefully tailored for the precise construction of seemingly seamless natural wonders. The author incorporated 3D scans of a man-made island in Bristol near the BBC's Natural History Unit as the backdrop to hybrid representations of the real and the speculative.

The Unnatural History Unit project asked questions on what nature really is, and through simulation, scanning, trickery and meticulous planning illustrated the extreme artifice of constructing ideal and false conditions to record phenomena that may only last for several seconds.

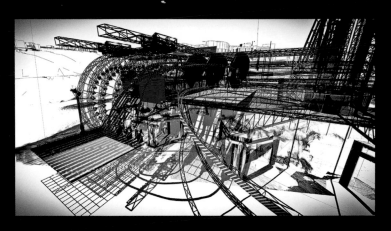

*Matthew Shaw and
William Trossell*

DIGITAL DOPPELGÄNGERS

FUTURE SCANSCAPES

Over the course of the last two years, ScanLAB
Projects have explored various fragments of the natural
and man-made world through the eyes of their forensic
measuring machine. From surface mapping of Arctic
ice floes in the Fram Strait (gateway to the Arctic) to
the documentation of torture and detention sites in the
Balkans, via the accidental editing of a Richard Long
sculpture, to purposeful acts of detail theft from Foster
and Wren. Here, **Matthew Shaw and William Trossell**
discuss the capture, analysis and refabrication of their
digital architectural doppelgängers.

ScanLAB Projects, Larkstoke Manor building survey, Cotswolds, UK, 2011
Lidar scan for Niall McLaughlin Architects as one of the first stages in a delicate and considered renovation and remodelling of this traditional Cotswolds manor house.

ScanLAB Projects, Private residence building survey, London, 2011
The forensic and uncanny level of detail captured by the lidar scanner offers not only unparalleled levels of survey information, but sometimes an uncomfortable invasion of privacy.

The act of bearing witness by machine is not new. Since early photography, a machine's-eye view of the world has acted as a means to convey a view to a remote audience. Even before this view could be translated to print, optical machines offered a more detailed view and an enhancement of that which can be seen by the naked eye. From the earliest microscopes and telescopes to modern remote sensing technologies that constantly remap the surface of the earth and the depths of space, it is mechanical observations that facilitate humankind's discoveries. Visuals from these machines are the evidence by which discoveries are shared with a wider audience. Lidar is one such technology and has enabled accurate spatial data collection in the fields of geomatics engineering, atmospheric physics, archaeology and the military since its conception in the 1960s.

The role of large-scale 3D laser scanning in architecture and design has less precedence, with its true value still emerging. With designers at the helm of this machine, focusing its view and staging the scenes it surveys, a more creative approach to landscape-scale forensics is evolving. Acting in the realm of point clouds, designers are using these digital records to provoke both 'site perfect' interventions and questions of precision. Existing among the plethora of digital design and fabrication techniques now available, this captured spatial data is evolving into physical constructs that are changing the way we understand and make spaces. It is also changing the way these spaces will be viewed and experienced in the future. In an increasingly virtualised world, architects need to redefine notions of site and adopt new tools of communication and representation such as lidar scanning.

The role of large-scale 3D laser scanning in architecture and design has less precedence, with its true value still emerging.

The Ultra Survey

As an evolution of the photograph, a lidar 3D scan freezes the dimensional properties of an object, space or event into a cloud of precisely measured full-colour points in space which can be revisited and inspected digitally, remotely and at any time. Traditional surveying techniques rely on human investigators accessing a space and measuring the dimensions of its volumes. Lengths are taken of important features at the discretion of the surveyor. A clear, organised, but limited picture emerges – the survey drawing. When decision making is handed over to a machine, these choices become less subjective and treated with equality: the distance from wall to wall holds no greater value to the machine's processes than the distance from wall to washing up, or to the crumpled cushion on a sofa. When a building is scanned, its occupation is surveyed, not just its bricks and mortar. The resultant cloud of information dissects a space, freezing it exactly at the time of the scan as a catalogue of use and an 'exactly as was' building model.

The physical act of scanning occupies its subject, establishing a grid of temporary and permanent references that calibrate the space and link individual scans together. While the laser is non contact, recording the surfaces it sees through an expanding sphere of laser pulses, traces of this act litter the physical world: survey pins, trig points, benchmarks, targets. They act as anchor points between the digital and the real, and hint at another version of space not seen in situ.

Forensic Vision

The same point-cloud software used to explore a building scan includes an automated blood-splatter analysis tool and bullet trajectory functions. The use of scanning at crime scenes and crash sites freezes clues securely in digital quarantine. It is forensic site examination, albeit at a larger scale, that has led to ScanLAB Projects' collaboration with Forensic Architecture, a research group run by Eyal Weizman and Susan Schuppli based at Goldsmiths, University of London. ScanLAB has added 3D scanning to an already abundant spatial vocabulary used by Forensic Architecture to reconstruct spatial scenarios. In the Living Death Camps project, Forensic Architecture and ScanLAB are using lidar scanning and ground-penetrating radar to tie together fragments of the past with the physicality and architectural reality of the present. The particular sites of interest are a Second World War concentration camp in Belgrade, Serbia, and a detention camp site near Omarska, Bosnia Herzegovina that was active during the recent Balkans conflict.

Increasingly it is physical scars across landscapes and cities that are used as evidence for the crimes of humankind. This evidence is observed not by humans, but by optical machines. On a landscape scale this forensic analysis of the earth and of past events often occurs using satellite imagery. In a strange parallel to early photography, the human is often not even present in this modern form of evidence. Not deleted through motion in a long exposure or removed by editing, but instead absent due to a lack of resolution. Forensic Architecture notes that the most readily available

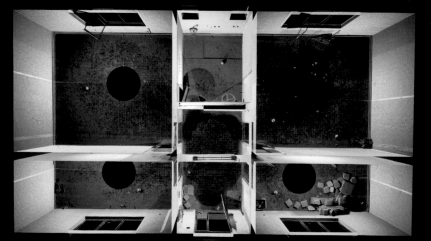

ScanLAB Projects, The LAB, Woburn Studios, London, 2010
The image represents an ongoing series of experiments to challenge
the scanners' perception of reality by scanning mirrored surfaces,
ephemeral cloud conditions and moving objects. The series charts
the resultant 'errors' and marvels at the blooms of contorted noise
and space created.

**ScanLAB Projects and Forensic Architecture, Living Death Camps,
The White House, Omarska, Bosnia and Herzegovina, 2012**
As digital memories, the scans of this former concentration camp
structure from the Balkans conflict act as the only access former victims
and their relatives have to this notorious site, due to its modern-day
function as a working steel mine.

and longest continuous space-based recording of the earth's surface, that collected by the Landsat Program, tends to have a pixel size on the ground of around 0.5 square metres (5.4 square feet), or approximately the space occupied by a human. So satellite imagery often cannot record the act of human suffering, only the evidence of this in alterations of the surface of the earth – machines observing the land and expressing the actions of man through the spatial trails they leave.

Measure on a Landscape Scale

The American West was once a wilderness to be conquered and tamed. One of the mechanisms for knowing and exploiting this vast terrain was to measure it. The pioneering expeditions of the American Geological Survey in the 1860s and 1870s sought to do exactly that, imposing a series of highly accurately known trig points as anchors to a system of order and understanding that was otherwise completely absent in the wild voids between.

A wealth of remote sensing technologies, including satellite imagery and aerial lidar, have begun to tackle these data voids in the US and globally, while mobile GPS means almost any point of the surface of the earth can become known almost instantly. There is a diminishing in size of the blank spots on the map and the voids in spatial data together with a simultaneous blurring between digital and physical realities. Scanning sits at the detailed end of landscape-scale information available, an emerging network of moments of precision delicately linked across the curved surface of the earth.

Digital Memories

The pressure to reach a wider digital audience and the quest to catalogue and preserve the world in the midst of both environmental and political turmoil are leading heritage organisations and museums to 3D scanning. A digitised version of a sensitive environment goes someway to making these artefacts and experiences available to all without the need to physically manoeuvre a troublesome public anywhere near valuable and delicate treasures. To observe or navigate a scan is to visit, or revisit, with uncanny, unnerving accuracy. The inclusion of the unimportant and the accidental only increases the notion that this is a perfect replica, and raises questions of value of the original versus the reproduction. When the digital double can be more readily available, digestible and accessible, the future of real archaeological ruins may be replaced by an immersive digital flythrough. When this information becomes so accurate that the archaeologists themselves find it easier and more successful to study remotely, this challenges the necessity and relevance of conservation.

Using a tool for its intended purpose under optimum conditions will produce a perfect, efficient result. Purposeful altering of these conditions and experimentation with 'that which may not work' has been the driving point for a series of recent ScanLAB projects that start to bend the scanner's perception of space or rematerialise the point cloud. A keen knowledge of the breaking point of technology is used in all of these experiments, pushing at the boundary and provoking moments of accident, surprise and delight.

Noise and the LAB

The LAB is an ongoing series of tests of the 'unscannable'. Terrestrial laser scanners operate within infrared or ultraviolet spectrums. These wavelengths behave in a similar manner to visible light, reflecting, refracting and absorbing depending on the materials they contact and the angle of incident. The LAB explores optical phenomena that are hard to pin down visually and that normally result in 'noise': unwanted, unreliable, untrustworthy readings. So-called 'stealth materials' that reflect or confuse the scanner's return signal are avoided in the everyday course of scanning, for the sake of accuracy and consistency. The LAB looks at the resulting blooms of false information, offset realities, distorted surfaces and data voids as a new form of space, only constructed when scanned.

The material subjects of these laboratory tests are part scientific and part ad-hoc collection; mirrored surfaces, mist, smoke, explosions, black glossy objects and mirrored disco balls find themselves paraded in front of the scanner in a pseudoscientific cataloguing of the unexplained noise. Objects are carefully positioned to act as shields or deflectors, carving the scanned reality of the laboratory space. Crucial to this process is the interruption of normal, automated processes of filtering and refining which increasingly dominate the digital postproduction of 3D scanned data in the manufacturer's pursuit of a 'user-friendly' automated process. Scans are stored and viewed raw, unedited, untidy, unusable.

Ultimately these material and spatial tests hint at future architectural scaled elements that will leave the LAB and occupy the city. When deployed, these elements will alter future digital versions of the cityscape by subverting data at its point of collection, introducing purposeful errors, voids and mistruths.

Increasingly it is physical scars across landscapes and cities that are used as evidence for the crimes of humankind.

ScanLAB Projects, Planar view of Swoon's *Murmuration*, Black Rat Projects, London, 2011
The artist Swoon creates imaginary cityscapes from discarded materials that are inhabited by her life-sized figurative wood-block prints. The images here illustrate how the scanner registers its position against geometric references and other scan locations.

ScanLAB Projects, Shipping Galleries, A Digital Archive, Science Museum, London, 2012
The entire Shipping Galleries, once home to the Science Museum's maritime collection, were 3D laser scanned before their decommission in 2012. The project was part of a collaboration with researchers from the Civil, Environmental and Geomatic Engineering department at University College London (UCL).

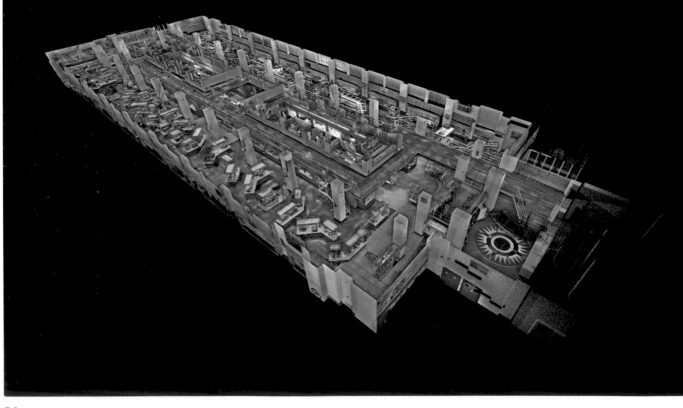

Copy/Paste

The Grand Stealth Tour & Great Detail Theft by ScanLAB @ UCL (the teaching wing of ScanLAB Projects at the Bartlett Schoool of Architecture, University College London) saw students undertake a covert tour of some of London's most notorious architectural monuments, from Wren to Foster. Over the course of a summer school workshop, and while avoiding the watchful eyes of the building's security personnel and the ever-monitoring City of London CCTV network, the students guided the laser scanner towards prominent structures. While students 'admired the architecture', the scanner mercilessly measured, captured and stored the buildings' details, cloning the original architects' intellectual property.

Post-capture, these scans were analysed for their accuracy; key details were zoomed into and extracted in preparation for unashamed replication. These open, publicly advertised acts of architectural piracy aimed to produce physical replicas made of cheap blue modelling foam, a purposely homogeneous 'nonmaterial' devoid of structural properties and accurate only in surface form. While removing the material properties, perhaps out of fear of prosecution for their blatant copying, these cloned fragments highlight the availability of technology that does exactly this, producing vast marble replica statues and columns, in the CNC workshops of Italy and Spain. While architecture is always referential, it is the 'copy/paste' nature of replication that is interesting here. These faux thefts question the delay of legal systems to fully understand and legislate for an architectural practice of highly accurate and automated scanning, analysis and replication – avoiding the design process and architects altogether.

A digitised version of a sensitive environment goes someway to making these artefacts and experiences available to all without the need to physically manoeuvre a troublesome public anywhere near valuable and delicate treasures.

Slow Life Scanning

The idea of skinning both a space and its inhabitation inform Slow Life Scanning, a series of carefully curated slow-motion figure scans. Originally a series of laboratory-style tests of timing and pace, these works now exist as a set of dialogues between past and present site-inspired movements. The arc of the scanner allows elongated exposure and multiplication of bodies. The skin of the figures is captured as it dances through 3D space, the shadows slicing the surfaces beyond. The latest performance of this technique took place in the underground cells of a former prison, the Clerkenwell House of Detention, in London. During a performance of *Macbeth* by immersive theatre group Belt Up, the labyrinthine tunnels became occupied by the fragments of past movements, tortured screams, and desperate hands scraping at damp bricks as moments from within the production were captured by the scanner. Individual limbs in motion hang forgotten in the hallways, the rest of the act disappeared.

In the next phase of these works, 3D skins will be cast from digital moulds of the scan traces. These physical props will be installed in the original space and performers will reinvestigate the exact positions of their former selves, touching the now cold bronze surface of the last time they were there.

Frozen Relic

ScanLAB's recent series of visits to the Arctic with Greenpeace and the University of Cambridge led to the staging of 'Frozen Relic. Arctic Works' at the Architectural Association's AA Gallery, London, in 2013. The content of this exhibition, the original 3D scans, originally fed extensive mathematical models of future sea ice levels in the Polar regions. This process squashes/data-crunches the three-dimensional nature of the scan into highly powerful, numerical calculations and predictions of ice formation patterns, average volumes, growth and melt rates. The spreadsheets are both mathematically groundbreaking and strikingly abstract from the month-long data-collection expeditions aboard icebreaker ships at 82 degrees North in the Fram Strait between the Svalbard archipelago and Greenland.

Frozen Relic reinvested this same data set with some of the material qualities of the original measured surfaces. In part a test of scale refabrication in an illusive material, ice, this installation also aimed to transplant a delicate landscape experience out of context and time, and into the gallery space in Central London. The fragments were exact in their detail, if only for the first few hours before the inevitable rounding of perfectly cast pressure ridges and melting of tiny replica footprints left the icy surface to become more abstracted, glowing, melting forms. A fresh installation of ice would plummet the gallery temperature, self-insulating for a while until the slow dripping of melt water filled the air and gradually the ice melted to collect in precisely dimensioned trays beneath.

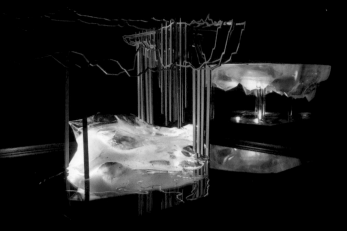

ScanLAB Projects, 'Frozen Relic: Arctic Works', AA Gallery, Architectural Association, London, 2013
'Frozen Relic' re-created the surveyed Arctic landscape in its natural material – frozen saltwater. Each piece was a digitally fabricated scale replica of an original ice floe that was 3D scanned from above and documented using underwater sonar from below to compile a complete 3D understanding of the ice.

ScanLAB Projects, 'Floe 006', Arctic expeditions, Fram Strait, 2011
This image shows the 21 individual 3D scan positions established to capture the top surface of this stadium-sized ice floe known as Floe 006. The morphology of ice floes affects their ability to withstand summer melting periods as temperatures in the Arctic rise.

Future Scanscapes

Lidar is one of a plethora of emerging tools that alter the way we design and view space. As architects adopt these tools, they become a part of the way we define space, and a catalyst for new ways to inhabit it. The intricacies of this technique, its accuracy and range, but also its error, mistake and shadows, will inhabit future catalogues of the world. The zoomable scanned encyclopaedias of spaces and events will provide exhilarating records of the past; maybe 3D scans will be the holiday snaps of the future. But digital versions of space will always be just that – exact lists of numbers, of x, y and z values, the experiential properties lost as pure data. The sound, temperature, slip and sudden cracking change of ice cannot be stored alongside the xyz value; the brush of damp stone on skin cannot be navigated by a left click or a zoom.

Scanning offers these challenges to designers. If a digitised version of space is uncanny yet cannot compete with the real, how can it enhance it, provoke it, change the way it is used? If a digital doppelgänger lacks the experiential character of the original, how can it provoke new objects and spaces that truly relate? Design demands inspiration and information, and 3D scanning floods a project with both. We look forward to provoking and charting its impact. ∆

Design demands inspiration and information, and 3D scanning floods a project with both.

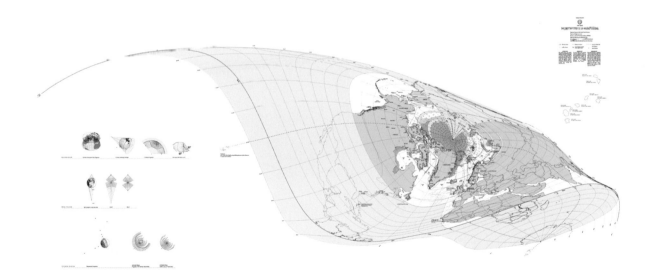

ScanLAB Projects, Arctic expeditions, Fram Strait, 2011–12
This drawing develops its own method of polar biased conical cartographic projection to locate a series of lidar-scanned ice floes captured as part of scientific expeditions with Greenpeace and the University of Cambridge.

*Ann-Sofi Rönnskog and
John Palmesino*

ARRAYING
TERRITORIES

**Territorial Agency, Multi-year spectral
analysis, Mirny, Russia, 2013**
Red 1999; green 2007; blue 2010. The
open-pit kimberlite diamond mine on Mirny,
closed since 2001, is at the centre of the
structures represented in this Landsat
data-derived image. Well after its closure,
vast changes in the tailings of the mine are
visible in red, green and blue in the lower
part of the image, indicating successive
expansion of the structures.

REMOTE SENSING AND ESCALATION IN THE NORTH

Founded by **Ann-Sofi Rönnskog and John Palmesino**, Territorial Agency is an innovative practice that advocates sustainable and integrated territorial transformations through architecture, research and action. Here, Rönnskog and Palmesino describe how their exploration of the shifting geopolitical conditions of the Arctic and subarctic regions has revealed an intensification of remote-sensing technologies and an escalation of military, scientific and industrial activities, which is resulting in 'a new landscape of agencies'.

Territorial Agency, Multi-year spectral analysis, Athabasca oil sands, Alberta, Canada, 2013
Red 1985; green 1998; blue 2011. The vast heavy crude-oil deposits in the sands in northeastern Alberta are rapidly being exploited: the largest deposits in the world suitable for large-scale surface mining are visible in blue, indicating the expansion of production over the last decade. Wide preoccupation with the impact of the mining and extractive complex has been expressed by First Nation groups, especially focusing on the proposed construction of a 64,000 cubic metres (2,260,000 cubic feet) a day pipeline to Edmonton in the south, and to the west coast port of Kitimat, British Columbia, by PetroChina and Enbridge. Less visible, in blue and to the east, are the prospecting fields to extend the operations further into the forest.

A series of intensifications are transforming the northern territories of the planet. The Arctic and subarctic regions are being reshaped into a new configuration where sovereignty, inhabitation, land, water and air are recomposed into a new architecture: a new set of active relations between polities and space.

The intensifications in the North reveal a complex mixture of operations, a new condition where measurement and vision technologies are shaping the architecture of inhabited spaces at unprecedented scale and amplitude. Automatic vision production technologies are rapidly becoming mediators of the deep transformations of the relationship between forms of material spaces and forms of the institutions that inhabit them.

Remote-sensing technologies, as well as a number of other environmental monitoring systems, are used in global change research, mining and prospecting, forest science, atmosphere studies, monitoring of sea routes, and military operations. While the object of earth observation images is often understood as spatial, it is the very multiplication of these images and the knowledge infrastructures they are linked to that mark the transformation of the North into a new architecture.

The multiplication of sensors sets out new territories with new boundaries, limits and frontiers. Measurement stations, remote-sensing missions, telecommunication relays, satellite earth observation, and direct measurement of the shifting environments of the boreal and Arctic regions, arrange a new set of devices for the delimitation of what is visible. They prepare the ground for the reorganisation of what was once a marginal space. All that can be measured is measured by a grid of interconnected sensors and operations that covers a tri-dimensional envelope that reaches from deep into the crust of the planet to the orbits of earth observation satellites.[1]

The architecture of these intensified territories is here seen as the process of construction and transformation over time of complex and expanded inhabited spaces. The architecture of the North is an extended active set of relations between territories and authorities, more than the sum of individual architectures, elements of construction, scientific settlements, fishing villages, routes and trails, pipelines, industrial outposts, military infrastructures and organisation of long-term inhabitation of the landscape. It is an organisation of both material and immaterial spaces. Climate-change science is both rooted in global modelling and measurement systems, and shapes the very environments it sets out to survey as it lays the foundation for an acceleration in the prospects of access to new resources. The automatic images produced to modulate, control, model and monitor natural resources and ecologies in the North form a new landscape: a simultaneous depiction and organisation of land. They are a bi-located landscape: at once above our skies and in the surface of the planet.

These intensifications present architecture with a demand to reconceptualise change and transformation: to what degree of magnitude can architecture operate?

A New Landscape of Agencies

The transformations in the North operate simultaneously at both global and local scales; they carve the surface of the planet and set a torque force on the links between individuals, small groups, corporations, NGOs, international institutions, nations and trans-local actors.[2] Open on all sides, the architecture of the North is a sensor of wide and amplifying transformations that are characterising the first decades of the 21st century.

The multiplication of remote-sensing technologies recomposes the image of the planet. Linking chains of causalities between natural processes and human intervention, they arrange a multi-scalar image, where discourses and practices linked to climate-change science and policy readdress many paths towards agency. While the main concept is one aimed at cohesive action, the interconnections of the new earth observation technologies and their wide use and multiplication imply a multi-directed arrangement of actors, initiatives, interests and visions. The new territories of the North are decentred and they multiply agencies. The North is conceptualised often as the ultimate horizon: the vast open expanse outside the metropolitan and industrial

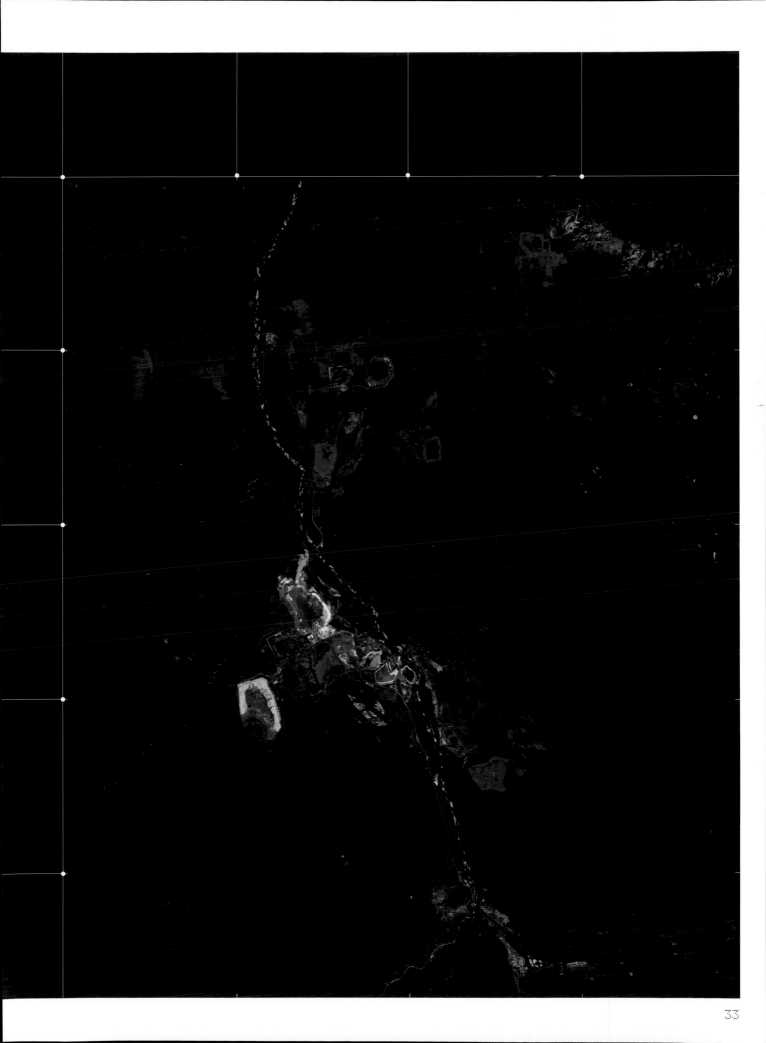

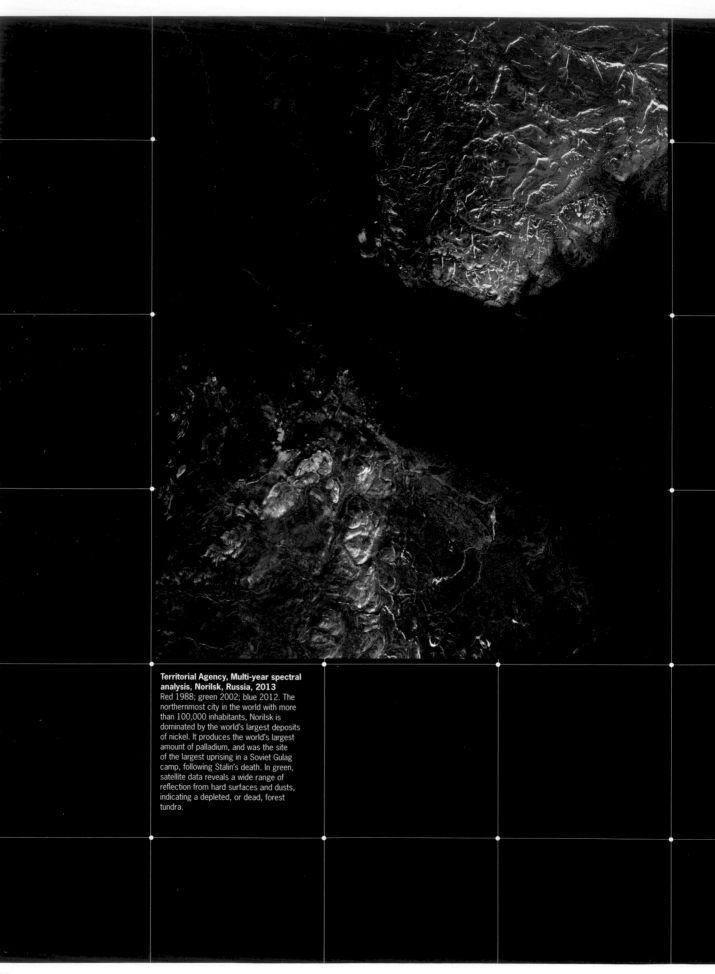

**Territorial Agency, Multi-year spectral
analysis, Norilsk, Russia, 2013**
Red 1988; green 2002; blue 2012. The
northernmost city in the world with more
than 100,000 inhabitants, Norilsk is
dominated by the world's largest deposits
of nickel. It produces the world's largest
amount of palladium, and was the site
of the largest uprising in a Soviet Gulag
camp, following Stalin's death. In green,
satellite data reveals a wide range of
reflection from hard surfaces and dusts,
indicating a depleted, or dead, forest
tundra.

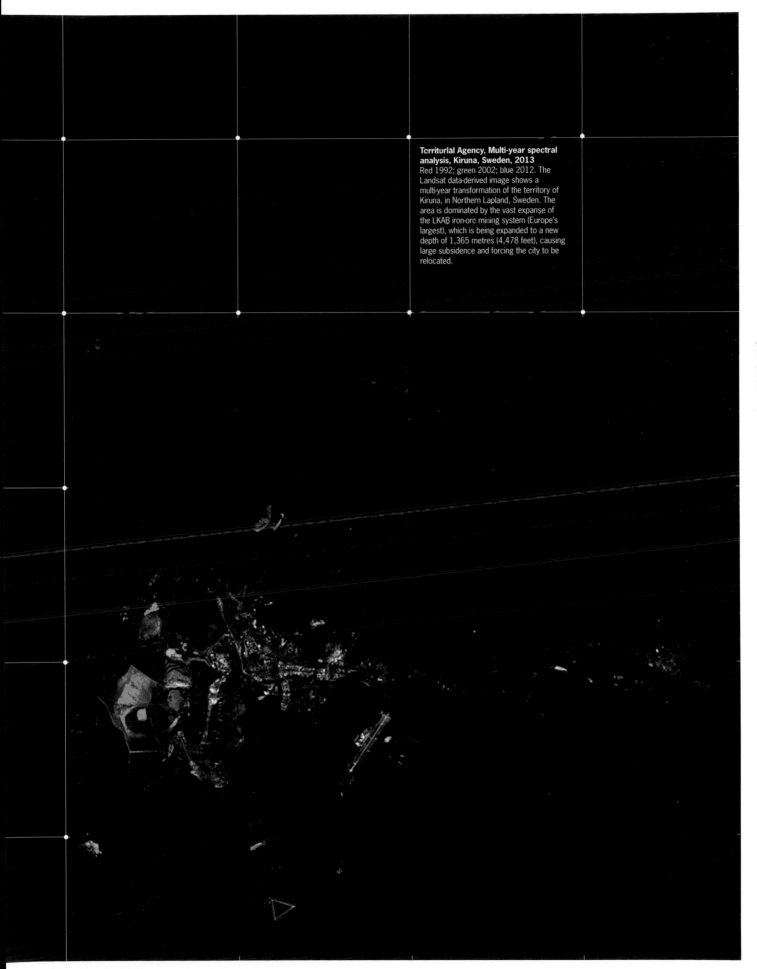

Territorial Agency, Multi-year spectral analysis, Kiruna, Sweden, 2013
Red 1992; green 2002; blue 2012. The Landsat data-derived image shows a multi-year transformation of the territory of Kiruna, in Northern Lapland, Sweden. The area is dominated by the vast expanse of the LKAB iron-ore mining system (Europe's largest), which is being expanded to a new depth of 1,365 metres (4,478 feet), causing large subsidence and forcing the city to be relocated.

Territorial Agency, Multi-year spectral analysis, Thule, Greenland, 2013
Red 1992; green 2002; blue 2012. Thule, in Northwestern Greenland, with its majestic glaciers, is the basis for a wide range of remote-sensing missions dedicated principally to the study of the Greenlandic ice sheet and mineral explorations. The Thule Air Base is the station for a series of synchronised National Aeronautics and Space Administration (NASA) and European Space Agency (ESA) flights across the Arctic Ocean, beneath the early-morning flyover path of CryoSat, an ice-sheet-measuring satellite, to link satellite earth observation with airborne data.

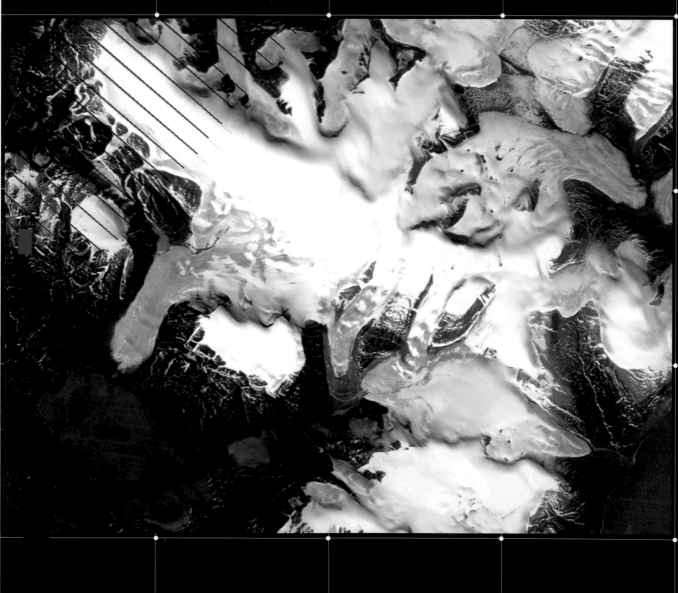

regions of the densely populated European, North American and Asian temperate areas: a vast and often unbounded concept of the Northern latitudes. Yet the new technologies and their proliferation of uses depict a landscape of expert practices and often exclusive rationalities, with multiplying boundaries and partition lines.

The North seems to operate both as an image of the unified and undisputed outside, and as one of intricate uncertainties, where the consequences of climate change open up new possibilities for access to natural resources and mineral prospecting. Yet these two images, one fixed and immutable – nature – and the other undergoing uncontrollable changes, operate simultaneously at all scales and levels of magnification. They exert a double shift that sets the North in a spin: an expansion towards a global and univocal predominance of climate-change practices and the reorganisation of the territories where action is carried out. The double image of the North is a bifocal condition where action is oscillating between an international space above the nation and a series of initiatives beneath the state: mining activities, new pipelines, transport infrastructures, organisation and control of herding, international monitoring of fishing, new science laboratories and missions, renewed military operations. The North is warped by this double image where horizons and close-ups cannot be accommodated within an overarching and stable organisation.

Remote Sensing: A New Technology of Borders

How to understand the measuring, representation and imaging of the Northern territorial intensities? What to make of the exponential rise in prospecting activities, in scientific measurement, and in the management of records and tables of natural resources? How to link the geopolitical reorientation to the transformation of spaces of inhabitation?

Technologies of vision relate authorities and sovereignties to their spaces of operation. They are the means through which architecture activates the relationship between contemporary polities and their material spaces. Measurement and monitoring technologies represent an almost primordial form of architecture: a technology that organises borders, links interiors and excludes exteriors.

Today, a new condition of visibility and a new set of borders are established by remote-sensing technologies: synthetic-aperture radar (SAR) sensors, gravitational measurement satellites, multispectral imaging, radio-magnetic measurement, microwave-radiometer sounding units, multi-beam sonars, scanning radiometers and angular radiance sensors. By organising margins of what is visible, they predispose land and sea for distribution of deeds, properties and concessions. They activate transformations in sovereignty, international law and trans-local assemblages of actors.

The new architecture of the North is a system of division, partition, demarcation and distribution. Imaging technologies reframe not only land, sky and sea, but also expert knowledge and sectoral rationalities. Each expertise acts on well-delimited portions of space and conceptualises change through clear-cut and exclusive view lines. The increase in measurement brings

about an increase in the differentiation and specialisation between the expert rationalities that are called upon to operate in the North. More measurements entail ever more prospecting activities and new technologies of vision and mapping.

The source and origin of remote-sensing technologies are predominantly to be found in operations research, Cold War game theory, systems analysis and earth systems, cybernetics and the apparatus of discourses of the early environmental movement. While their origin implied a rationale of scientific calculus and integration, the space they have opened up is one of discordance, accelerated divergence, competing and multiple interests. The polar view of the United Nations flag and of the distant alert system for intercontinental ballistic missiles of the Cold War era, envisioned a North torn between competing superpowers. It was a North where access to knowledge was modelled through vast arrays of computers and simulation software. Yet that unified image was just one. There was still the possibility of conceiving the escalation of thermonuclear conflict as a complex warfare communication system, where there was an overall rationality, and where decidability was operational, governed as it was by game theory and complicated arrangements of strategic options.

Contrary to the unified and integrated image of bilateral conflict produced by escalation as a military strategy, and its computational technologies, a new kaleidoscopic image is formed by the ambivalence of climate-change science, of the mineral industry, of biosciences, as well as renovated military regional alliances and threats. It is a double image that never allows the possibility of a complete recomposition of the shards and splinters of contemporaneity.[3] The wide system of formation of global data and of global monitoring does not provide a unified space of authority. Rather, it opens up and tears apart the links between local procedures and stabilised territorial conglomerates. There is no one institution that operates access to knowledge centrally. Availability of resources, meeting demands and preferences are no longer elements of calculation for planning. They become elements of a complex calculus machinery which is non-localised, interconnected and dispersed, and acts without any general coordination.[4] It is a space where agency seems more linked to a casuistry than to an overall viewpoint.

Escalation

In a pattern reminiscent of the conflict architecture of the Cold War, escalation seems to be the dominant theme of today's transformation processes in the North.[5] Transformations and new activities, from military to scientific and industrial, are announced at an increasing rhythm. The North is a complex and often contradictory arrangement of transformation processes. Here, non-synchronised change and multi-directed initiatives pose continuous questions on the focus and cohesion of action. Exemplary local change ranges from increased access to navigation in the Beaufort Sea, to the Shtokman Project in the Barents Sea; from oil sands extraction works in northeastern Alberta, to the extension of pipelines in the North Slope of Alaska; from the deformation and subsequent relocation of the city of Kiruna in Swedish Lapland induced by the LKAB mine extension, to the extraction of rare earths in the Kola Peninsula; from the Alcoa aluminium smelting facilities in Greenland to vast acidification and deforestation in the boreal regions; from contested military presence in Canadian waters to the reorganisation of road networks in permafrost areas of Arctic Russia.[6]

More than a multiplication of differences between regions, the North is a simultaneous intensification, an expansion of the number of actors and an acceleration of differentiation processes. The architecture of the North is a multidimensional transformation process: rarely it appears as a stable set of engagement rules and spatial ordering.

Ensconced by a spin that expands concerns to the planet earth, and extends and multiplies actors across borders, the North presents us with a wide range of experiments in reorganising the relationship between polities and spaces. The new intensive architecture of the North implies a wide reorganisation of authority. The Sami transnational parliaments in Scandinavia of the past decade, the Self-Government Act of Greenland in 2009, the new October 2012 constitution in Iceland, the Nunavut Act and Nunavut Land Claims Agreement of 1999, the trans-border region of Kirkenes, the Scottish independence referendum of 2014, are experimentations into a new form of mixture: a coalescence of human agency with high-tech monitoring systems.

The North is carved, wrought, punctured, inscribed and modified in its material body and surfaces. More than by the extraction procedures of hyper-industrialisation, which forms the main counterpart to the image of immaculate nature, the North appears to be reshaped by the multiplication of remote measurement and imaging. Its architecture is not contained in stable forms and recognisable inhabitation structures. Contemporary form-generating activities and practices rely heavily on calculus and automatic image production to control their spaces of operation. Interlinked as they are, and crossing multiple disciplinary borders, these automatic images are reshaping the polities and the territories of the North – they are reshaping its architecture.

The contemporary escalatory transformations of the North can only be accessed through the complex relaying systems of remote-sensing technologies and the global data of climate-change modelling. What architectures are then laid out? Who is the author of the transformations in the Arctic? Where is its authority?

A New Architecture

The contemporary transformations of the North are a new surface, a new land, in intensity rather than in extension.[7] The new architecture of the North is a new augmentation of nature. The radical transformation of the surface of the planet is conducted through the transformation of circumpolar, trans-local and international polities and the manifold procedures and practices tied to remote-sensing technologies, audits and surveys.

The slightest modifications of the surface of the planet are revealed by the Landsat earth observation archive datasets, analysed in their multispectral radiation of the surface of the earth. The magnification of transformations is what is relevant: intensity sets off balance the spatial configuration of contemporary spaces. Small areas appear semi-stable, wide expanses enter into rapid mutations. Scanning the surface of the planet for more than 40 years, the Landsat programme, a wide US and international scientific project launched in 1972 with the Earth Resources Technology Satellite, represents the largest archive of earth observation, an archive constantly updated, queried, reorganised and reprocessed, and is the main resource for global-change research.

The materials that form the surface of the earth in the Northern regions are mapped and analysed in their transformation processes. Acquiring new data at each orbit, the Landsat sensors detect the radiation reflected and emitted by the earth's surface. As different materials have different reflective capacity, the multiple sensors of Landsat allow for an analysis of the composition of the materials forming a specific portion of the planet. From its polar and sun-synchronous 99-minute orbit at an altitude of 705 kilometres (438 miles), Landsat takes 232 orbits, or 16 days, to scan the entire surface of the earth. The multi-year analyses of transformation shown here are produced from data from this archive. Sounding the spectrum between the frequencies of 0.45 and 0.52 micrometres, the electromagnetic reflections detected by the Landsat multiple sensors depict the transformations in the hard and semi-hard surfaces. These

Nikel, Kola Peninsula, Russia, 2012
View of the Norilsk Nickel plant. Once part of Finland, the town of Nikel is dominated by the heavy contamination produced by the smelting plant, which produces 90,000 tonnes of sulphur dioxide per year.

impervious surfaces constitute the substrata, the infrastructure of human activities. The images portray the material evidence, the reconfiguration of the surface of the planet, of the intensified activities in the North. A new series of form-generating processes are brought into vision, and a new set of sectoral and expert rationalities projects boundaries of expertise and margins of action.

Can architecture supplement the grid of rules, criteria, protocols and laws that characterises the showcasing of human intervention at the higher latitudes, by integrating spatial analysis with image making, geographic knowledge and remote sensing? How to think about new parades, processes and processions where knowledge production, measurement and survey are intertwined with the forming of inhabited territories? What can architecture achieve in these new territories? How can it shape them? Can we re-imagine these new lands and waters of intensities, yet not assume a central position in their conceptualisation? Can architecture engage other form-generating practices in new radical negotiations? Can architecture rethink its agency?

In the North, territories are arrayed; they are prepared for a new, intensified set of transformations. And the thesis of this new geological epoch – the Anthropocene – is being tested and tried through the many procedures and practices of measurement and image production. ∞

Notes
1. Pavel Kabat, director of the International Institute for Applied Systems Analysis (IIASA), in conversation with the authors, June 2013.
2. Saskia Sassen, *Territory Authority Rights*, Princeton University Press (Princeton, NJ and Oxford), updated edition, 2008.
3. Bruno Latour, 'Facing Gaia: Six Lectures on the Political Theology of Nature', Gifford Lectures, Edinburgh, unpublished manuscript, 2013.
4. Paul N Edwards, *A Vast Machine*, MIT Press (Cambridge, MA and London), 2010.
5. John Palmesino and Ann-Sofi Rönnskog, 'Escalation', in Steven Kovats and Thomas Munz (eds), *Deep North*, Revolver Publishing (Berlin), 2009.
6. In 2012, John Palmesino, Ann-Sofi Rönnskog and Armin Linke were part of fieldwork that took place in the Kola Peninsula, Russia, organised by the Oslo School of Architecture and Design (AHO Oslo) with support from the Norwegian Research Council, and additional support from Forensic Architecture, a European Research Council (ERC) project at Goldsmiths, University of London.
7. Bruno Latour, Interview by the authors, *Anthropocene Observatory*, Haus der Kulturen der Welt (Berlin), 2013.

Zapolyarny, Kola Peninsula, Russia, 2012
View of the Norilsk Nickel mine. Norilsk Nickel is the largest diversified mining and metals company in Russia, the world's largest producer of nickel and palladium, and one of its largest producers of platinum, rhodium, copper and cobalt. The mine is the site of the Kola Superdeep Borehole, a scientific experiment of the Soviet Union to drill as far as possible into the earth's crust, reaching 12,262 metres (40,230 feet) in 1989: the deepest hole ever drilled.

TRACKING, TAGGING AND SCANNING THE CITY

Andrew Hudson-Smith

James Cheshire and Ed Manley, Twitter Languages in London, The Bartlett Centre for Advanced Spatial Analysis (CASA), University College London (UCL), 2013
Twitter mining along with machine text analysis opens up the ability to map a city's languages, illustrating its diverse nature in geographical clusters.

The proliferation of social media and software, such as building information modelling (BIM), has led to an unprecedented accumulation of data in the last few years, which can be tracked, tagged and scanned. With it, buildings and cities have been transformed into portals for information. **Andrew Hudson-Smith**, Director at the Centre for Advanced Spatial Analysis, University College London (UCL), describes how the ability to use emerging urban analytic tool kits provides the possibility of a real-time view of the city and a crystal-ball-like glimpse into urban networks of the future.

Fabian Neuhaus, Mapping Twitter Locations in London, The Bartlett Centre for Advanced Spatial Analysis (CASA), University College London (UCL), 2011
Tweets can be collected and mapped to reveal the hidden social networks of the city.

We are emitting an ever-increasing amount of information into the built environment. Every day we create 2.5 quintillion bytes of data; 90 per cent of the data in the world today has been created in the last two years alone. This data comes from everywhere: sensors used to gather climate information, posts to social media sites, digital pictures and videos, purchase transaction records, and mobile phone GPS signals to name a few.[1] Through this data, buildings and cities are becoming portals for information, and at the heart of it all is the ability to track, tag and scan information. From the hyper-local tagging of individual components in building information modelling (BIM) systems through to the tagging of individuals via social networks, almost everything has the ability to radiate information. These streams of data that cities and individuals emit can be collected, visualised and added to predictive modelling systems. The use of emerging urban analytic tool kits opens up the possibility of not only a real-time view of the city, but also, via trend and sentiment analysis, a predictive insight into the future of urban networks.

Social Networks

Social networks are currently one of the most prolific data sources; every minute, 100,000 tweets are sent globally, Google receives 2 million search requests, and users share 684,478 pieces of content on Facebook.[2] An urban phenomenon – from 'check-ins' with Foursquare through to Twitter 'tweets' and 'likes' with Facebook, we are constantly sharing information with the wider world. While many would like to think that this information is kept between our followers or friends, in reality the terms and conditions of many social network sites mean that our data can be collected, mined and viewed by anyone with knowledge of application programming interfaces (APIs). It is not only the textual or pictorial information that can be collected, but also location. An increasing amount of this data stream emitted by cities and individuals is geo-located, and can be collected and mapped to visualise an invisible data network.

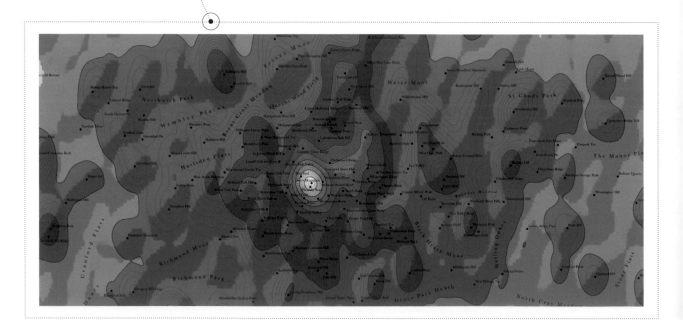

A number of geographic features can be highlighted in the data, for example transport hubs, as each tagged tweet has a location and time stamp.

By running multiple cloud-based servers, software can collect data, en masse, with the capability to archive hundreds of millions of tweets every hour on a global scale. This opens up a mass of information – 'big data' – and with it the ability to change the way we view the city. By way of example, it is possible to map the language of the city, extracted from over 3 million tweets, using Google Translate software. Detailing the density of languages in London, the grey foundation of the Twitter Language map illustrated here is formed from the majority English tweets. Other languages can be picked up in specific locations, for example to the north of the city are blue (Turkish) tweets, and Arabic (green) tweets appear around the Edgware Road. Finally, Russian-language tweets (pink) are of note around Central London.

The use of social networks is a conscious decision by an individual, yet increasingly almost all of our interactions in the city are being tagged and tracked. The use of Oyster cards to pay for journeys in London is one such example. You can swipe your card at any Underground station to see your recent journeys; multiply this by all the travellers on the network and you have a time-stamped view of flows around the public transport network. Simple spatial analysis allows the visualisation of flow volumes of the Tube network at their morning peak based on a data set of all journeys in London over a period of six months.

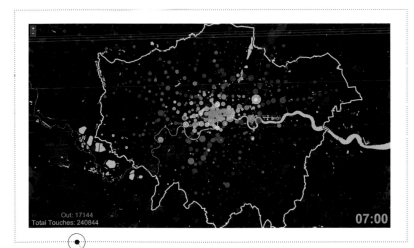

Oliver O'Brien, London's Oyster Card Flows, The Bartlett Centre for Advanced Spatial Analysis (CASA), University College London (UCL), 2012
Visualising all the touch-in and touch-outs of the system.

Urban Data and the Internet of Things

Over the last few years there has been a sea change in the availability of data. Where once the landscape was clouded by terms of use and issues around ownership, it is now becoming a much more open environment. The London Datastore[3] is one example; a download data service from the Greater London Authority (GLA), it stands out as one of the first steps towards opening up data related to the city. It was developed with the ethos of allowing anyone to access the data held by the GLA and other public-sector organisations and to use it however they see fit – for free. To date, it has stimulated over 70 mobile applications linking to its 500+ data sets and combinations of its 27 real-time live traffic and data feeds.

The key to opening up our understanding of the city is the joining of such data sets with other feeds and systems. The collection and visualisation of live data linked to current systems such as the established BIM and geographic information system (GIS) sectors, and the emerging Internet of Things (IoT) movements, is central to this ethos. The 'Internet of Things', a term attributed to the Auto-ID research group at the Massachusetts Institute of Technology (MIT) in 1999, denotes the idea that in future every object will have an online presence.[4] Information from occupancy rates through to ambient temperature can be collected using sensors linked to the IoT; combined with location and time attributes, it moves from the hyper-local view of the sensor through to the macro scale of an urban system. The IoT is still in its infancy with systems ranging from the Xively public cloud and an array of numerical data, through to Tales of Things (of which UCL's Centre for Advanced Spatial Analysis/CASA is a collaborator) and its narrative-based take on objects (see below). It is estimated, however, that over 6 billion objects will be connected to the Internet by 2015.[5] These tagged and tracked objects will form the backbone of future smart buildings, information systems and, ultimately, the smart city, for data analysis, predictive modelling and visualisation.

Scanning a second-hand item using the Tales of Things mobile app is effectively tagging second-hand goods moving inside the city space. Tales of Things, funded by the Digital Economy Research Councils UK, allows any item to be tagged and tracked over time with its history attached, enabling it to communicate its past and allowing its current history to be recorded. Such tagging and scanning means an object's full lifecycle can be recorded, from production through to ownership, resale and, ultimately, to waste. Tales of Things provides a glimpse of a future where every item is connected via its ownership and location, creating a new layer to the city's infrastructure that includes its history. For example, a wall next to the Roundhouse events venue in Camden, London, was once host to *The Chambermaid*, one of the most notable works of the graffiti artist Banksy, which was subsequently painted over by Camden Council.

However, scanning a tag that was placed on the wall by a local resident loads up a panoramic view of the wall circa 2007. This ability to scan a tagged item in the city allows anyone with a mobile phone to pan around the actual location and view a historical capture of the space.

Smart Citizens

Such applications rely on crowdsourcing, or citizen science. As Muki Haklay states, 'using citizen science can take a form in which volunteers put their efforts into a purely scientific endeavour, such as mapping galaxies, or a different form that might be termed "community science", in which scientific measurements and analysis are carried out by members of local communities so that they can develop an evidence base and set action plans to deal with problems in their area'.[6] Largely driven by the rise in mobile phone ownership and access to networked technology, 'the crowd' is both a provider and user of data. Many crowdsourced applications are still only in prototype stages, but with the ability to ask a crowd to share their location, as they move across a city, they have core implications for urban event management and policing.

Key examples include a live capture by SIS Software of crowdsourced location data during the Lord Mayor's Show in London in 2011. Here, the aggregated data of all participating visitors is used to create a real-time overview of crowd density at an event location. Organisers can then use the system's output to identify potential hotspots before they turn into hazards. Situations can thus be defused by sending visitors location-based advice either via a push notification or SMS text.[7] Volunteered tagging is similar in nature to adding location to your social network traffic; it allows a new generation of data miners and data scientists to collect and map your location, opening up the view of the hidden city.

We are of course already trackable via our home address or details linked to more traditional forms of data. Any data that includes an address or postcode can be linked. One extreme example is the arrest location of offenders compared to their home addresses during the period of the riots that occurred across London during August 2011. Such snapshot data-views are becoming increasingly possible by simply using social network data. Mining social networks for key words and applying sentiment analysis, linked to location, it is possible to gauge the mood of a city and to predict where and when future unrest could occur.

Andrew Hudson-Smith, Banksy in Camden, The Bartlett Centre for Advanced Spatial Analysis (CASA), University College London (UCL), 2008
Panoramic capture of a now lost urban space, reinstated using QRCodes and the Internet of Things (IoT).

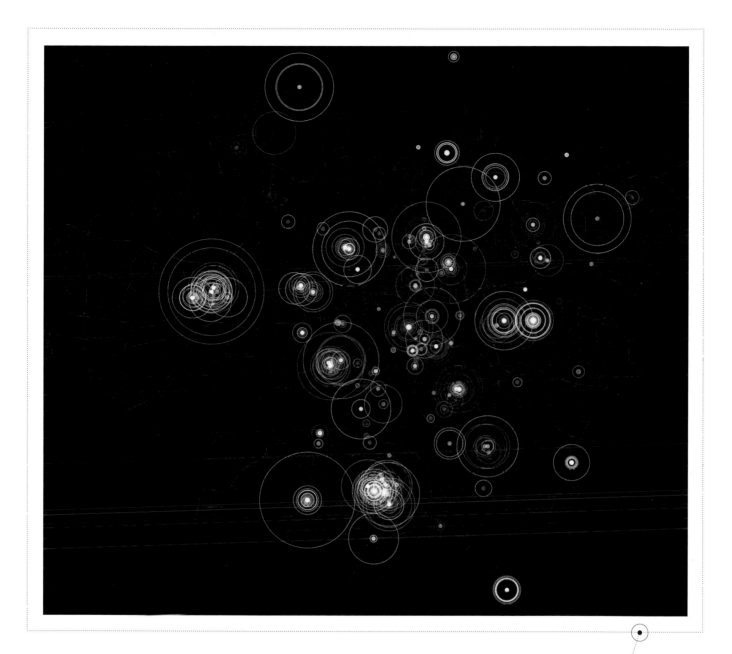

Mining social networks for key words and applying sentiment analysis, linked to location, it is possible to gauge the mood of a city and to predict where and when future unrest could occur.

Shane Johnson and Martin Zaltz Austwick, Tagging and Tracking the London Riots, Department for Security and Crime Science, The Bartlett Centre for Advanced Spatial Analysis (CASA), University College London (UCL), 2012
The combination of an offender's postcode and the location/time of the crime provides a spatial view of the August 2011 London riots.

Once data is released it can be collated and analysed, enabling the visualisation of patterns and complexity across space and time. From networked objects through to the movement patterns of a crowd, emotions and criminal activities, the ability to tag and track changes how we view the city. It also shifts how we view the network of urban space. For example, anyone with knowledge of data science can access the timetables of all public transport routes, not only city wide, but national, and this is now moving towards global coverage. With a series of geographic links, the data can be merged to provide a visual image of a city's transport system, such as the 114,000 daily bus trips made in London, allowing a clear picture of bus coverage and detailing its importance to the network operations of a city.

The live data behind the bus routes can be used to display not only the locations of all the buses on the network, but also network capacity and number. With the increase in live data feeds, a different view of the city is required. As standard map-based visualisations quickly reach capacity, a more general view of the data is required. One such example is the display provided by CASA's CityDashboard (www.citydashboard.org), which was developed as a way of not only collating but also simplifying the city data-gathering and visualisation process.

CityDashboard not only displays data; it also acts as a data collector, allowing for later analysis and analytics. The dashboard currently has in excess of a billion tagged data records and has moved into physical form via a 3 x 4 iPad wall. The City Wall, a customised version of the dashboard based around 12 iPads, was built specifically for the Office of the Mayor of London to provide a view of data across the city. Using the touch capacity of iPads, it allows data to be viewed either direct, or by tapping a screen to obtain a historical view.

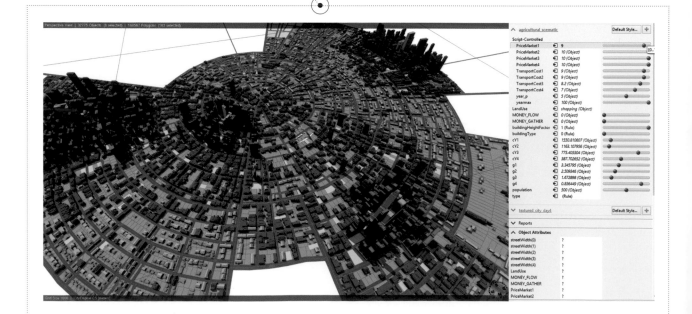

With an increasing number of data sets coming online from the increasing use of the IoT, citizen data and systems such as the GLA's Datastore, the next challenge is not only storing and making sense of the data, but also feeding it into urban modelling systems. With such data feeds it is possible to measure the performance of a city and build predicative analytics via background urban models operating in real time. With applications from transport planning through to the measurement of urban resilience, the emerging tagged and tracked city is one of a macro to micro scale that can also adapt to data and model outputs.

Feeding data into geographic information and four-dimensional modelling systems, such as Esri's CityEngine, has the potential to create a true live representation of the city, where 'what if' questions can be asked based on tagged, tracked and scanned data. We are only a few steps away from being able to zoom into the city and see any one of the 6,000 buses on their real-time path within a three-dimensional cityscape. Every building is already tagged with historical data; it simply needs to be connected to the IoT and wired into the network. BIM linked to GIS, and in turn linked to real-time feeds and the public at large, is arguably the next step in creating an intelligent urban system that makes sense of the vast amount of incoming data.

Technology moves rapidly, and at the moment it is the mobile phone that acts as the interface, the collection point and disseminator of the majority of not only social network data, but also that relating to built form. In order to use a mobile phone, we need to take it out of our pocket, look down at and type into, arguably, a device that is now time limited. Within the next decade the mobile phone will likely be defunct, with systems such as Google Glass and inevitable iterations bringing augmented reality to the forefront of data collection and viewing the city. With the ability to tweet, take a photograph or update Facebook via voice command or a blink of the eye, augmented reality systems have the potential to truly change the way in which we view the city. As such, we are moving towards an era of 'always being on', where tracking, tagging and scanning will simply be taken as given. For those interested in the built form, it will finally be a way to find out how people use, feel about, work, live and play in smart buildings and, ultimately, the smart city. ◠

Notes
1. IBM, 'Big Data at the Speed of Business', 2013: www-01.ibm.com/software/data/bigdata/.
2. Mashable, 'How Much Data is Created Every Minute?', 2012: http://mashable.com/2012/06/22/data-created-every-minute/.
3. http://data.london.gov.uk/datastore/about.
4. Martin de Jode, Ralph Barthel, Jon Rogers, Angelina Karpovich, Andrew Hudson-Smith, Mike Quigley and Chris Speed, 'Enhancing the "Second-Hand" Retail Experience with Digital Object Memories', *Proceedings of the 2012 ACM Conference on Ubiquitous Computing*, Pittsburgh, Pennsylvania, 2012, pp 451–60.
5. Anita Bunk, 'The Internet of Things – New Infographics', January 2013: http://blog.bosch-si.com/the-internet-of-things-new-infographics/.
6. Muki Haklay, 'Geographical Citizen Science: Clash of Cultures and New Opportunities', in (Proceedings) Workshop on the Role of Volunteered Geographic Information in Advancing Science, GIScience, 2010.
7. SIS, The Lord Mayor's Show, SIS Software, 2013, http://www.sis-software.co.uk.

CityDashboard, The Bartlett Centre for Advanced Spatial Analysis (CASA), University College London (UCL), 2013
Visualising live city data feeds in near real time via a tablet-optimised dashboard places instant city information in the hands of the general public.

Within the next decade the mobile phone will likely be defunct, with systems such as Google Glass and inevitable iterations bringing augmented reality to the forefront of data collection and viewing the city.

Ilona Gaynor and
Benedict Singleton

Ilona Gaynor and Benedict Singleton, founding partners of design and research studio The Department of No, look beyond the specific technological possibilities of acute accuracy and explore the principle of zero tolerance as an aesthetic of precision. How is such an aesthetic at work when an architectural strategy places a heightened emphasis on the exact placement of objects in space and time? Could the precision in which a single spatial intervention is pursued have more fundamental and far-reaching consequences than we ever imagined?

WHAT WE WANT IS IN THAT ROOM

As architects know well, there is a certain pleasure to be found in a thing well made. This pleasure is so simple, it seems, that it does not warrant further investigation. Architects find little point in discussing the obvious fact that, without a certain minimum degree of precision, a building does not stand up. Likewise, that one can be pleased to come across a structure that holds together apparently against the odds – the work of a designer that has brought ingenuity and finesse to their craft – seems too basic, too obvious, to draw comment. But it is a pleasure about which there is more to say.

The Department of No's interest in this very particular kind of pleasure is piqued by the tranche of newly developed technologies to which this issue of $\triangle$ is dedicated. These technologies comprise systems for scanning environments and modelling the processes within them, to historically unprecedented

Ilona Gaynor, Everything Ends in Chaos, 2011
Film still: the board members in deliberation while a bomb hangs above their heads.

levels of detail. Of course, such systems, and the increasingly acute spatial interventions they permit, find a wide range of applications. They offer new resources to, say, those interested in the optimisation of wing surfaces, rifle bores or chip architectures. They unlock new constructive possibilities through novel material arrangements at the nano scale; the extraordinary conductive, optical and mechanical properties of a one-atom-thick graphene lattice is one example.[1] And they help to construct strikingly new spatial situations. Consider, for example, the military contractor VAWD Engineering's 'life form detection' system, which exploits new radar technologies to 'see through' architectural obstructions and identify, by their heartbeats, the human targets they conceal.[2]

The purpose of this essay is not to prospect the architectural potential of one, or a group of, these technologies. Its interests lie elsewhere. If these technologies implicitly posit a principle of zero tolerance as a horizon architecture can approach, it invites an exploration of this principle as such – an aesthetic of precision as a quality of design in general, not the precision afforded by a given system or technology. The following discusses how this aesthetic is at work when architectural stratagems are given force through exact placement and timely action. In these situations, the precision with which a single spatial intervention is made can turn a world on its head, creating, undoing or transforming the whole.

The Aesthetic of Precision
An aesthetic of precision connects architecture with other fields, and can offer a point of transit between them. If architecture hones an appreciation for the arrangement of material in space and over time, this appreciation can extend to forms other than those taken by buildings. Within the very same register – highly materialist, mechanical, geometric – one can appreciate the deft hands of the pickpocket or a surgeon as much as those of the architect.[3] Indeed, architects perhaps have more to learn than to teach in this regard – in the first instance from film, where the use of detail to mobilise a plot is a staple device.

Among many possible examples, David Fincher's *Panic Room* (2002) stands out for its rigour. The film's minimalist premise is that three men break into a Manhattan townhouse, believing it unoccupied. A mother (Jodie Foster) and daughter (Kristen Stewart), who moved in that day, take refuge in the fortified panic room of the film's title, not knowing the intruders are after a fortune in bearer bonds in a concealed safe within their haven. The film documents the increasingly desperate measures taken by the invaders to get into the room, and by its occupants to get out. The structural geometry of the house goes beyond mise-en-scène and becomes a protagonist in its own right; the phrase that titles this essay, 'What we want is in that room', is written on card and held up to a closed-circuit camera in one of many moments in which highlights and textural details become integrated into the

plot, as a set of coordinates and portals that locate, differentiate and connect the house's rooms. The drama hinges on plug sockets, phone lines, ventilation shafts, wall cavities and other domestic infrastructure, which become vital components in the siege as means of entrance and exit. The camera moves unimpeded through the house's architecture, smoothly passing through walls and doors, following the lines of pipes and telephone cables, rendering the action in slow, perfectly linear pan shots that focus on the details of space, material and surface as pivots in the plot.

Everything Ends in Chaos
Panic Room is predicated on the ideas that spatial precision grants access to environments previously off limits, and that apparently incidental details and subtle interventions can produce outsize effects. These ideas are key to an expanded architectural aesthetics of precision. *Everything Ends in Chaos* (2011) investigates these ideas through very different means.[4] It reverse-engineers a fictive global financial catastrophe, tracing the intricate trajectories of people and things implicated in the unfolding disaster, in ways that are cinematic, but that narrative film disallows. It began as an attempt to design a 'black swan', a term popularised in Nassim Nicholas Taleb's book of the same name, in which it stands for an unpredicted event that makes a massive impact.[5] The image itself is an older philosophical saw,

Scenario map and artefacts. A chronological index detailing the twists and turns of events.

Ilona Gaynor, Under Black Carpets, 2012–
Scale models: bystanders, witnesses, police,
women and children, and hostages.

relating to the encounter with black swans by the first Europeans to reach southern Australia. Before then, every swan they had ever seen was white; but the generalisation 'swans are white' was wrong, despite all the evidence hitherto.

The project's plot begins with the kidnapping of the wealthy wife of a senator, Mrs Henderson, which sets in motion a series of events that accumulate to create a global economic disaster. Working with bankers, brokers, loss adjustors and risk strategists through the course of the project, the scenarios depicted were passed through actual actuarial assessment as to their probabilities and financial implications. The project investigates the points at which economic and architectural fact collide with speculative fiction – those of actuaries assessing future probabilities as much as those of designers; and explores, too, the various modes of precision that are at work, from insurers' assessments of the value of individual body parts in the case of their loss or destruction, to the specific location of people and devices in a series of environments that allow the catastrophe to emerge.

This plot is communicated through a collection of objects, diagrams and narrative texts to articulate the course of events. Its final scenes – among them a flight of doves that have been fed Mrs Henderson's diamonds escaping forever through a limo sunroof, and a golden commemorative missile exploding in a boardroom – are presented through film. The connection between the spectacular image on film and the technical infrastructure that produces it is not incidental. Technologies of cinematic production provide a critical reference point for this architectural aesthetic. Precision does not only obtain a well-rendered final product, but also encompasses the devices that go into creating it; that is, the systems that allow precision to be achieved – strategies and techniques of modelling events, imaginative rehearsal, the speculative entertainment of multiple possibilities. Film production, and its contracts, meetings, scale models, test footage, shot lists, schematics, maps and timelines, is an art of coordinating the objects and processes that must come together with precision to yield a single image.

Under Black Carpets

These devices share a striking similarity with those used in another field where an aesthetic of precision is paramount: forensics. Many contemporary technologies lend themselves to the deconstruction of events into a probabilistic topography of actions, one that can be deployed before a jury to argue fact and intent: found footage, microscopy, ballistics diagrams, DNA swabs, 3D laser scans, satellite imaging and more. These technologies lend to forensics not only a portfolio of diagnostic means, but also a substantial aesthetic force.[6] In the courtroom, exactness translates into plausibility, which in turn is the currency of persuasion. Which is to say that, no matter what the facts of the case, precision produces legal agency through the suspension of disbelief.

Under Black Carpets (2012–) is an investigation into the relationship between architecture and law, crime and forensics.[7] It presents a fictional event – the simultaneous robbery of five different banks in the area around One Wilshire in downtown Los Angeles – through a set of objects to be used in court. In this case, the objects, from alibi reconstructions to trajectory diagrams, are 'evidence' that is not recovered from the scene, but created for the express purpose of activating a conclusive legal discussion. As such, they do not seek to produce a definitive map of the events that occurred, but something that looks beyond reasonable doubt, estimating probabilities and plugging gaps. Precision serves both sides here: the intricate techniques used in the robberies to gain access to vaults and make good on the getaway, and the authority's efforts to produce a retrospective picture of events that is persuasive enough for a sentence to be passed, even if it is false.

The Physics of Power

As in Everything Ends in Chaos, there is no straightforwardly moral directive to Under Black Carpets. They are projects that attend to 'a physics, not a theology, of power'.[8] They do not aspire to conjure images of some kind of utopia in the hope of inciting architecture towards it, or for that matter posit a dystopia to be evaded. Instead, they

Ilona Gaynor, Under Black Carpets, 2012–
Model artefact: an American Airlines A300 domestic carrier plane is dropped onto One Wilshire to serve as a chaotic distraction.

pursue an examination of the mechanisms of risk assessment, financial calculation, and rather more literal, legal forms of judgement – abstract systems that undergird societal structures and are powerful forces of architectural production in themselves, generating new situations as fast as a handshake or as slow as a building. To explore them is to invoke an aesthetic of precision that foregrounds the risk of precise architectural action – what is gambled in narrowing margins of space and time, where exactness matters and becomes a force in its own right. The easy-going amorality that comes with appreciating a technical feat for itself becomes something different when intensified to this point, where visceral situations are coupled with the unflinching detachment that their complexity requires, and acumen – literally, sharpness – becomes the deciding vector. The principle of zero tolerance is unforgiving of error. ᴆ

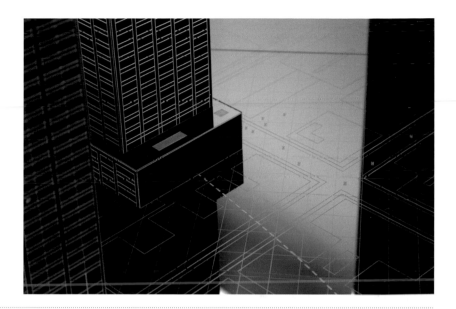

Model detailing: markings highlighting the trajectory of the American Airlines A300 vessel as it hits One Wilshire.

They [the projects] do not aspire to conjure images of some kind of utopia in the hope of inciting architecture towards it, or for that matter posit a dystopia to be evaded.

Notes
1. See http://en.wikipedia.org/wiki/Graphene#Properties.
2. http://vawdengineering.com.
3. See Robert Friedel, *A Culture of Improvement*, MIT Press (Cambridge, MA), 2010.
4. Everything Ends in Chaos, by Ilona Gaynor: see www.ilonagaynor.co.uk/Everything_Ends_In_Chaos.
5. Nassim Nicholas Taleb, *The Black Swan*, Penguin (London), 2001.
6. Eyal Weizman, *The Least of All Possible Evils*, Verso (London), 2012.
7. Under Black Carpets, by Ilona Gaynor: see www.ilonagaynor.co.uk/Under_Black_Carpets.
8. Grégoire Chamayou, *Manhunts: A Philosophical History*, Princeton University Press (Princeton, NJ), 2012.

Model detail of carrier hotel, One Wilshire, the building that serves as a target for distraction.

Birgir Örn Jónsson, Islands of Vision, Lee Valley Regional Park, London, Unit 23, Bartlett School of Architecture, University College London (UCL), 2012
The tool aims to be a hybrid between a scaled representation and a full-scale mock-up in direct relation to the viewer.

Birgir Örn Jónsson

DRAWING INTO THE CLOUD

Architectural designer, maker and researcher **Birgir Örn Jónsson** describes Islands of Vision, a speculative design project that he developed while in Unit 23 at the Bartlett School of Architecture, University College London (UCL). Acknowledging the predominance of the image and the underutilisation of the full range of visual experience in contemporary life, Jónsson set out to explore the entire field of vision, reasserting the periphery 'as a rich and dynamic mode of sensation'. With the aid of ScanLAB Projects and their 3D point cloud scanner, Jónsson scanned the project's site at Lee Valley Park, East London.

There was another oil painting hanging above the desk … If you watched the straight lines of the schooner's masts and rigging long enough in the dim light of an early evening or on a rainy day, the sea would begin to move at the corners of your vision. They would stop the moment you looked directly at them, only to slither and snake again when you returned your gaze to the ship.
— Paul Harding, *Tinkers*, 2009[1]

The act of seeing seems so natural that it is difficult to appreciate how constructed and malleable it really is. As writers such as Juhani Pallasmaa, David Michael Levin and others have observed,[2] visual perception in contemporary life seems to be strongly characterised by a foveal character of vision, at the expense of the full range of visual experience. We see the world increasingly through interfaces, and it gets mediated back to us as images. This affects the way in which we engage with our surroundings. Similarly, architects must always deal with representation, because we work to scale. But the thing that is represented can be veiled by its manner of appearance.

Architecture is predominantly conceived and drawn with tools that address only a portion of the visual field, be it screen, model or sheet of paper. The fovea constitutes the central two degrees in our horizontal field of vision, the bit that we are looking *at*. It deals mainly with objects and detail, whereas peripheral vision is concerned with the question of 'where', and the gathering of stimuli to form a spatial hypothesis of our surroundings in concert with the other senses. Our computer display generally sits right in our foveal vision. As the screen becomes our window to the world, this becomes a problem. We make judgements about what we are looking at based on the physical presence of the representation – its proximity and scale in relation to us in space – as much as from the thing that it represents.

The projected grid allows for convenient notations in the visual field.

Islands of Vision

Developed in Unit 23 at the Bartlett School of Architecture, University College London (UCL), Islands of Vision is a speculative design project that seeks to treat the entire field of vision, and the periphery in particular, as a rich and dynamic mode of sensation. The title is borrowed from Scottish ophthalmologist Harry Moss Traquair, who described the visual field as an 'island of vision … surrounded by a sea of blindness':

> Immediately within the coastline … smaller objects are visible and colours can be recognised if in large enough patches, and as the neighbourhood of the summit is approached smaller and smaller objects become apparent until at the apex of the pinnacle the most minute details can be detected.[3]

The project envisions a field laboratory for spatial perception in a semi-natural segment of Lee Valley Regional Park in East London. An assembly of architectural attractors, obfuscators and scintillators is choreographed in relation to an observer as he passes through. Some of these skirt the edges of his vision, while others hide in his blind spots at set points in the promenade. Their aim is to constantly turn the attention of the observer from what is in front of him to what is around him. Thus he is encouraged to witness himself seeing, and by so doing is dislocated from the centre of his own gaze.

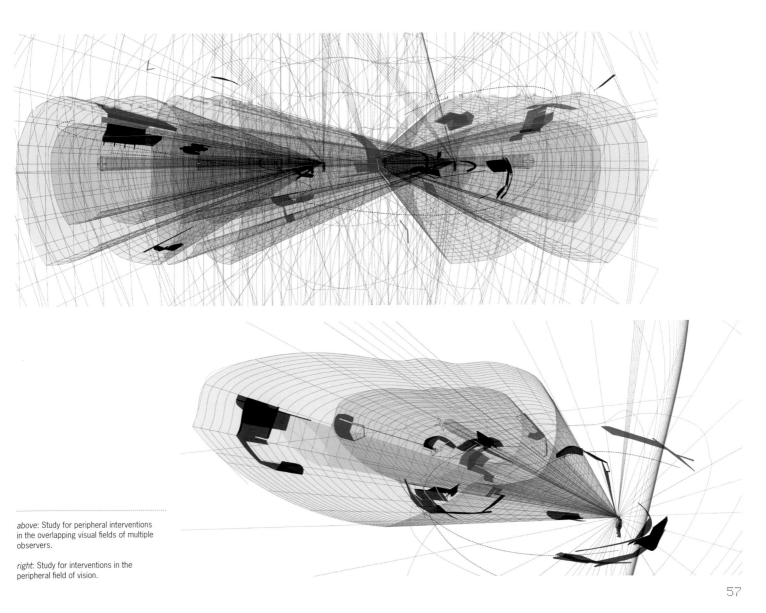

above: Study for peripheral interventions in the overlapping visual fields of multiple observers.

right: Study for interventions in the peripheral field of vision.

It is difficult to interrogate a space that deals with the periphery from a mode of representation that excludes peripheral vision, and so the project was developed through the making of tools that cater for the dynamics of the visual field in the design process. Key areas in the visual field were modelled at full scale in order to test ideas and relationships between components, and to see these close to how they would appear to an observer. The tools encouraged the juxtaposition of models at different scales according to their position in relation to the viewer.

What the Scanner Sees
The site in Lee Valley Park was 3D-scanned with the generous assistance and insight of ScanLAB Projects. This has proven to be a pivotal turn for the project, firstly because of the wealth of information that the point cloud offers, and because the scanner itself is an inspiring model of vision. The gyrating eye of the scanner focuses on everything at once and therefore nothing in particular. It is only when the point cloud has to be represented on a picture plane that it becomes arrested by means of projection that focuses the observer's eye on a focal point.

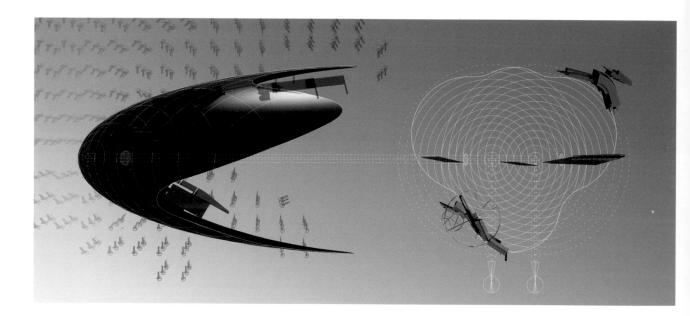

The tools encouraged the juxtaposition of models at different scales according to their position in relation to the viewer.

Components appearing and disappearing from the observer's field of vision as he passes through the scheme.

The manner in which point cloud 3D scanning records space and matter should therefore open up a wealth of new approaches towards architectural design. For example, there is a long-established tradition of conceiving and describing architecture in terms of lines, volumes, surfaces, planes and other forms of geometric abstraction. Abstractions are of course precisely that – they relate to conceptualisation or means of designing (the ease by which one defines a border by putting down a line, for example), but less so to human experience or the reality of material in its rich heterogeneity and subjection to external forces. But point cloud scanning delineates space with an unforgiving accuracy, picking up the minutest variations in material. Instead of assuming that the built world is a maze of objects sharply defined by borders and vectors, the point cloud describes a world that is an immensely rich field of almost limitless difference and variation. It offers a way to think about spaces and forms more in terms of saturation and density, similar to peripheral vision, which deals less with form than the fovea does. This is perhaps more tuned to our spatial perception in natural environments, in which we lose our focal points and lines of reference in favour of a heightened peripheral awareness.

An architecture that caters for peripheral vision provides a key to the other senses, and a means to empower the observer, as it demands more engagement on his behalf. Because representation tends to rely on the foveal, the design approach needs to be informed by experience and perception. The designer must, by focusing, create and define things that are not meant to be focused upon. ᴆ

Notes
1. Paul Harding, *Tinkers*, Bellevue Literary Press (New York), 2009, p 32.
2. See, for example, David Michael Levin (ed.), *Modernity and the Hegemony of Vision*, University of California Press (Berkeley, CA), 1993, and Juhani Pallasmaa, *The Eyes of the Skin: Architecture and the Senses*, John Wiley & Sons (Chichester), 2005.
3. Harry Moss Traquair, 'Essential Considerations in Regard to the Field of Vision: Contradiction or Depression?', *British Journal of Ophthalmology*, February 1924, p 50.

The design tools were developed by projecting sections through the visual field into a dome that corresponds to the retina's gradient of acuity.

LANDSCHAFT

REVISITING *THE JOURNEY* AND *DRIVE-IN HOUSE*

For visionary architect and founding member of Archigram **Michael Webb**, high definition has become a lifetime's pursuit. It represents the distillation and layering of material and meaning in ongoing works that explore the same theme over space and time. Here he discusses two projects – *The Journey* and the *Drive-In House* – which he commenced in 1977 and 1987, respectively, and that he continues to the present day; they express his essential preoccupations with his home landscape and the perfect contour of the car.

Michael Webb, *The Journey: Studies from the Temple Island Project*, 1977– *opposite*: 'Greetings from Henley'. The modified postcard used for the *Temple Island* gridded perspective studies. The pyramid is shown truncated by a horizontal cut parallel to the plane of the river and a vertical cut perpendicular to it. The cuts allow the negative shadows to burst through the surfaces of the cone.

Ice core. Plan/elevation combo of the regatta course. It is 8pm on 2 July 1949. Weather: 32°C (90°F). Wind: calm. I have allowed myself the notion that the air within the cone has magically solidified. It can thus be removed from the overall landscape and investigated independently like an ice core. My easel is located outside the ice core. My foreground is the camera's background. So the volume of air I paint must show an inversion of the normal colour gradient of the evening sky. It is therefore shown as cerulean blue around the camera's foreground, and orange around my foreground. Oil on gessoed particle board (work in progress).

Two projects, both motivated by a certain personal longing: the first, *The Journey*, a wish to embark on an unrealisable pathway whose beginning point is the location of the photographic film placed in a 1930s camera, and whose end point is the vanishing point of the perspective projection the film records.[1] The second, *Drive-In House*, a longing for the perfection of contour achievable in a car body and its likewise extension of that perfection into the architecture of the house it serves.

LANDSCHAFT[2]

A landscape dear to one, perhaps through long association, does tend to entice those happy few among us who draw and, as they say, capture it. And when using the word 'capture' they probably mean that through some alchemy, the drawer has persuasively flattened on to a two-dimensional surface an as yet unperceived, and maybe even fugitive, essence of the three-dimensional subject. But to capture is also to take possession of, not in the real-estate sense of owning title or even of occupying it militarily, but instead through the 'grokking'[3] of it that drawing brings. The landscape in question is that of the regatta course at Henley-on-Thames;[4] namely, the volume of air, land and water enclosed by a perspectival cone of vision[5] whose axis is parallel to the plane of the river and whose apex is in the Cyclopean eye of the beholder. I have allowed myself the notion that the air within the cone has magically solidified. It can thus be removed from the overall landscape and investigated independently like an ice core. Thus, the cone becomes the site for an imagined journey that this text attempts to describe. See Figure 2.

2

My easel is in a location other than that of the camera, however the painting depicts only what the camera can see; meaning that only objects within its purview may be featured. What lies behind those objects will appear, from my chosen vantage point, as negative 'shadows' radiating from the camera lens: voids slashing through the ice-core sky, water and ground. Were the camera to be moved, the voids would start rotating like movie gala searchlights; they would create new gashes in the surface of the cone. To locate oneself somewhere within this landscape of mobile caesurae would present an evanescent spatial experience. The overall image would thus be decidedly unconventional. Now see Figure 3.

Around the vanishing points in Figure 4 exist a domain of extraordinary line compaction increasing until, at the points themselves, the compaction becomes infinite. You might be forgiven for thinking of a black hole – or rather, in this case, a black slit out of which nascent grid lines are constantly pouring. At least this would be the impression when travelling towards it. To approximate a diagram representing a black hole one would need, paradoxically, to be moving way from it; that is, the grid lines would then appear to be sucked into the hole's maw. By contrast, the domain around you, the observer, is one of line distension, increasing until, at your actual location, the distension becomes likewise infinite. So look at the grid lines extended forward: the grid squares, as a result, become ever more lozenge shaped until they approximate (but never achieve) a flattened, parallel condition. Decidedly disturbing therefore is the implication that you, the observer, are infinitely far from the observed, which suggests the following paradoxes: in a plan projection the observer and the vanishing point are infinitely far apart; in a perspective projection itself they are coincident. A condition exists of equal but opposing symmetries: of compaction and distension, a sort of inverse symmetry of the near and the far, of the observer and the vanishing point.

bottom: Plan/side view of mobile stadia and their shadows. Adjacent to the finish line are located two floating stadia that swing round at the appropriate moment to offer the spectators a continuously optimal view of the finish. Their own negative 'shadows' create mobile gouges out of the river. Coloured overlays on illustration board.

3

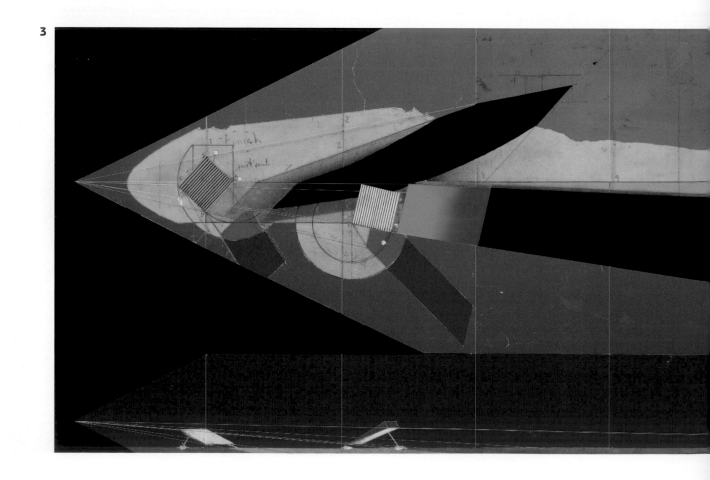

right: Perspective projection of two horizontal grids (1977 version). The perspective projection of two limitless horizontal square grids (Figure 5) was done in 1977 as a response to the then prevailing orthodoxy at the Cooper Union, New York, that anathematised perspective. Ink on tracing paper.

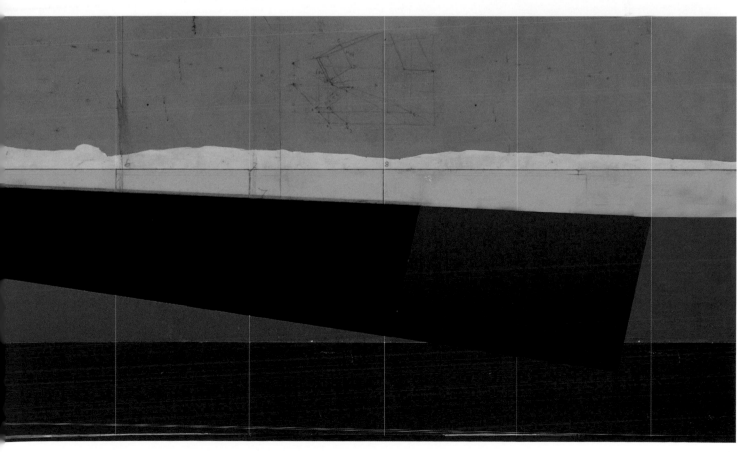

In Figure 5 the density of lines creates an edge to the compressed domain that seems to vibrate. I do not have a clue why, but the case for the black hole is made less ridiculous by pretending that what we are observing is not a perspective, but an orthographic elevation. A vertical section is then drawn perpendicular to the picture plane so that it intersects the horizon halfway between the vanishing points. The section indeed seems to indicate that the grids now curve asymptotic to the implied horizon. Now the problem arises of how to show the extent of the section cut when the paper on which it is printed is of finite size. Can this cockpit of the sheet of paper hold the vasty (sic) fields of France?[6]

Perspective projection of two horizontal grids (2010 version). Coloured inks on paper.

5

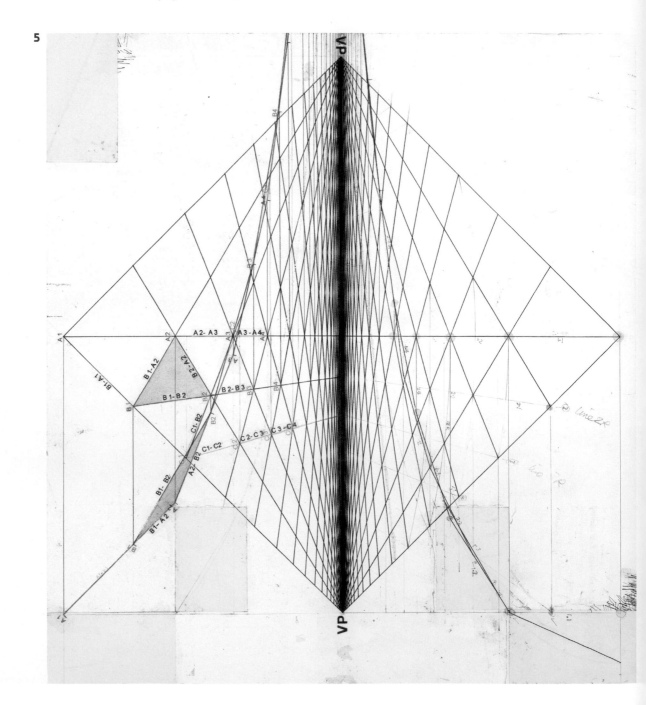

Section/perspective combo of the regatta course. To make a perspective in days pre-digital, one had perforce to first draw a plan projection from which the perspective could then be constructed; ergo: the two systems are structurally connected. Just how connected is apparent in this digital drawing where the perspective of the regatta course is placed alongside the plan so that line one on the perspective extends line one on the plan.

THE JOURNEY

With *Siegfried's Journey to the Rhine* from *Die Götterdämmerung*,[7] or the journey of despair undertaken in *Die Winterreise*[8] in mind, I conceive of an epic[9] journey from the observer to the vanishing point. Let it be assumed that the beginning point of the journey is the location of the camera lens, and that the vanishing point occupying the centre of its visual field is the end point. The beginning point cannot be shown in the perspective projection, nor the end point in a plan projection of the same. The route will be along the axis of the pyramid of vision.

The journey may be understood either as a venturing into the implied three-dimensional space of the pyramid of vision or as the actual traversal of the two-dimensional surface of the photographic emulsion depicting the pyramid. Figure 6 is part orthographic plan and part perspective projection of the regatta course. I have divided the course into 23 equal parts. By constructing diagonals the position of lines 2 to 24 in the perspective may be ascertained; line 24 in the perspective miraculously extending line 24 in the plan. The diagonal constructed from line 2, intended to establish the position of line 0, shows that the latter cannot be positioned because it is parallel to the regatta course.

Let us now imagine a point moving at a constant velocity over the surface of the photographic emulsion from O the camera lens to O the vanishing point occupying the centre of its field. Now further imagine that the point, travelling at the same velocity and following the same route, is instead to be understood as venturing into the three-dimensional domain the emulsion depicts. Now it will appear to be accelerating, but at what rate? Figure 6 diagrammatises the journey: if the point takes, let us say, one minute to traverse the distance between each subdivision in the plan projection, then, since the intervals become foreshortened in the perspective, it will take progressively less time to traverse them.[10]

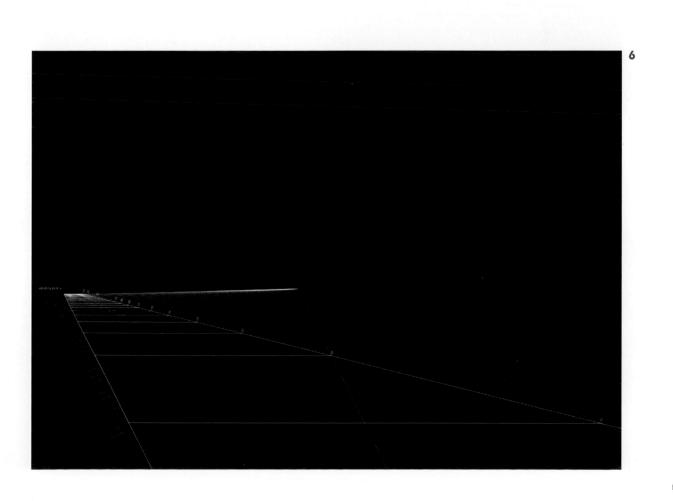

6

With *Siegfried's Journey to the Rhine* from *Die Götterdämmerung*, or the journey of despair undertaken in *Die Winterreise* in mind, I conceive of an epic journey from the observer to the vanishing point.

Spatial/temporal plan projection of the regatta course. Oil on gessoed particle board (work in progress).

For example, between lines 24/01 (the finish line) and 12/13 (Figure 7)[11] there are 12 equally spaced subdivisions each 100 metres (328 feet) long. If they take one minute each to traverse the point, they will obviously take 12 minutes to arrive at 12/13. Its velocity will be 1,200 divided by 12 = 100 metres (328 feet) per minute, or 6 kilometres (3.7 miles) per hour. In the perspective projection, though, there is only one subdivision between 24/01 and 12/13, and so the average velocity of the point will appear to be 0.5 kilometres (0.3 miles) per hour.

PARTIAL TABLE OF VELOCITIES

	plan projection (km/hr)	perspective projection (km/hr)
24/01 to 12/ 13:	6	0.5
12/13 to 08/17:	6	1.5
08/17 to 06/19:	6	3.0

7

The length of the subdivisions may be understood either as pertaining to space or to time. If the latter, then when read as spatial the dimensions must be stretched or compacted to fill the space allotted to them. The wavelength of light will likewise be stretched or compacted; a bias towards the red end of the spectrum at the beginning of the journey and towards the blue at the end. There is, of course, a sweet spot in between where space is neither stretched nor compacted; where the landscape appears identical to its depiction on the other side of the river. All this has been the means by which I have grokked this dear landscape.

Michael Webb, *Drive-In House*, 1987–
top: Side elevation of a customised, stripped-down Lamborghini. Oil sketch on gessoed illustration board.

bottom: Initial schematic design for *Drive-In House*, shown as a heat diagram. Four-phase horizontal section cut. Color-aid paper on illustration board.

8

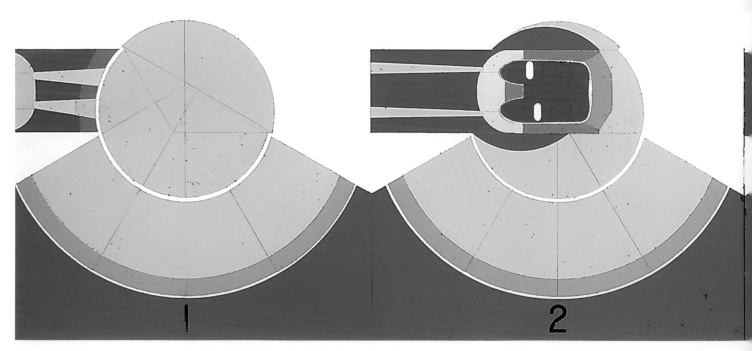

DRIVE-IN HOUSE

The motor bus rushes into the houses which it passes, and in their turn, the houses throw themselves upon the motor bus and are blended with it.[12]

I first recall the revelation of Reyner Banham upon his arrival in the US from the late 1960s onwards, that what he identified as really interesting was not the essentially urban and urbane work of the likes of Mies van der Rohe, IM Pei, Paul Rudolph et al, but rather the indigenous ex-urban world of drive-ins and mobile homes. '[A drive-in movie theatre is] just a flat piece of ground where the operating company provides visual images and piped sound, and the rest of the situation comes on wheels. You bring your own seat, heat and shelter as part of the car. You also bring Coke, cookies, Kleenex, the Pill and god-wot (sic) else they don't provide at Radio City.'[13] This

is a world described in *The Geography of Nowhere* (1993) by James Howard Kunstler with a far lesser degree of bedazzlement.[14] The auditorium is the major spatial volume of a theatre. It must be heated, cooled and cleaned. When the people are gone, so is the building.

Figure 9 suggests what a rudimentary drive-in house might look like, done as a heat diagram so as to try and suggest that the car, by entering the empty shell of the house, becomes an energiser. The headlight beams, for example, hit reflectors bringing light to that bedside table etc.

1. ...'tis night: warm car enters cold access tube.
2. Cool drum rotates anticlockwise to allow warm car to enter cool drum.
3. Cool drum rotates clockwise to enclose warm car.
4. Wall of drum seals interior from frigid exterior, so that doors can begin opening.
5. Axis of warm car aligns with that of house, doors now fully open.

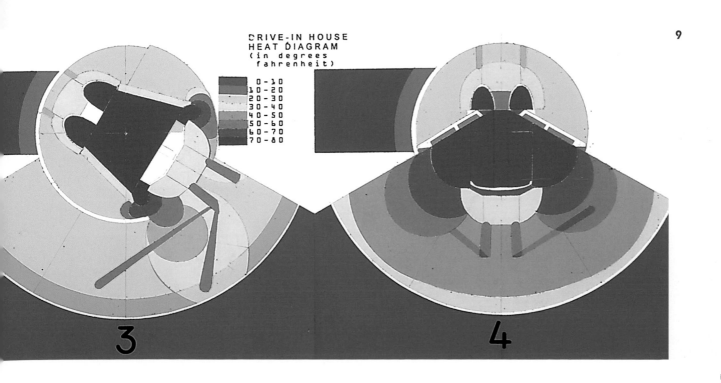

DRIVE-IN HOUSE
HEAT DIAGRAM
(in degrees
fahrenheit)

0 - 10
10 - 20
20 - 30
30 - 40
40 - 50
50 - 60
60 - 70
70 - 80

9

3

4

Imagine sitting in one's car parked inside an all pressed-metal garage while wearing a suit of armour. No longer to be viewed as three concentric but unrelated skins, the possibility of close, even intimate connections between them maybe presents itself to the unruly mind.

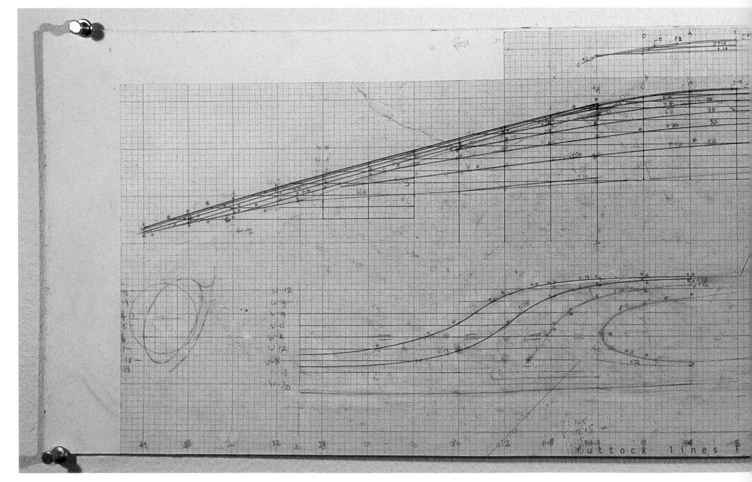

Imagine sitting in one's car parked inside an all pressed-metal garage while wearing a suit of armour. No longer to be viewed as three concentric but unrelated skins, the possibility of close, even intimate connections between them maybe presents itself to the unruly mind. Such led to the imagery depicted in Figures 10 and 11. Figure 10 being a 'lines drawing'[15] of the severely modified Lamborghini car depicted in Figure 8. Such a detailed formal description of the car body was necessary in order that the above-mentioned intimate connections could be engineered – see Figure 11.

Michael Webb, *Drive-In House*, 1987–
'Lines drawing' of car. Ink on graph paper.

10

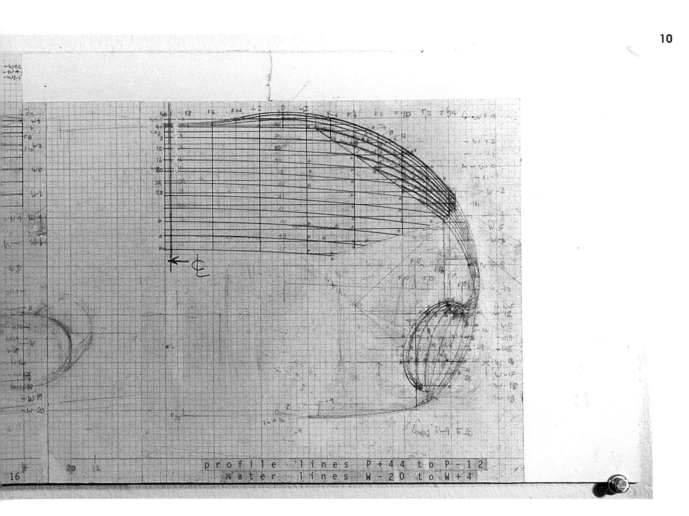

I wrote back in 1972:

Wasteful and sad, though, that out there in the 'burbs the mobile component of vita domestica sits out on the driveway or in a parking lot unused for most of the day. Luxuriously appointed interior with crushed velour seats, surround radio, hi fi, TV and cocktail cabinet, the car is swankier than the house interior to which it is supposedly ancillary.[16]

NEW JERSEY AS A LINEAR STRIP OF LAND EITHER SIDE OF A HIGH-SPEED ROAD

Webb to architecture student at the New Jersey School of Architecture:

'What town do you live in?'

Student:

'Oh, you get off at Exit 17.'

His presumption that I will know what I have to get off of, my presumptions as to his mental map of the Garden State, reminds me that the world of drive-ins – his world – while foreign to me, is rich with potential and green too.

Both projects presented here, developing slowly over time, continue to explore the relationship between representation and the represented. In the context of the theme of this issue of Δ, they reflect on the evasive qualities of capture and observation, and offer the navigator an intermediary chart into the wonders of the unrealisable. Δ

Three-phase horizontal section cut. Obeying the convention of placing the main entry of a building along the bottom edge so that one enters 'up' the drawing, the driver's line of sight is likewise 'up' in all three phases, meaning that the building must rotate around the driver rather than the driver around the building. Color-aid paper, airbrush and solar path diagrams on illustration board.

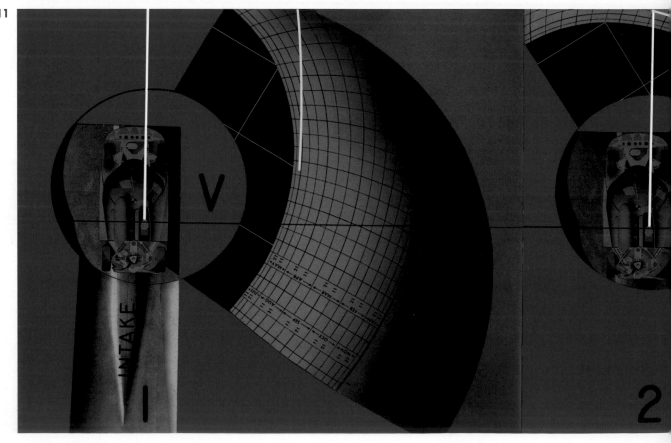

11

Notes

1. The test bed (aka site) is that of the regatta course at Henley-on-Thames.
2. A genre of painting focusing on the landscape as subject matter appropriate for a work of art. Using the German word here sounds somehow more academic.
3. A word invented by Robert A Heinlein, the so-called 'dean of science fiction'. It appears in his book *Stranger in a Strange Land*, Putnam Publishing Group (Kirkwood, NY), 1961. The somewhat pale *Oxford English Dictionary* definition is to 'understand intuitively or by empathy; establish rapport with'. The sense of the word conveyed in the book has no synonym in our language; thus its demise is lamentable.
4. The author was born and grew up nearby.
5. The cone of, or rather, as in this case, the pyramid of vision, is merely a device of perspective drawing to prevent the subject from appearing distorted by making sure its mass lies fully within the pyramid. Were a peripheral field vision (PFV) test to reveal such a narrow field, advanced glaucoma would be the diagnosis. Since the observer cannot see beyond the limits of the cone, according to the quaint rules of perspective projection, all is black nothingness outside it. The hats worn by the ladies suggest that the photograph was shot in the 1920s, implying almost surely the use of photographic film. The image would thus have been rectangular and the three-dimensional space revealed pyramidical.

6. The question refers to the chorus (in the quarto editions the word 'chorus' is not used) in Act 1 of *Henry V* (1599) by William Shakespeare, whose chorines muse as to whether the vast battlefields of northern France can be adequately represented on the tiny stage of the Globe Theatre.
7. An orchestral interlude from Wagner's music drama (1876) describing young Siegfried's journey in search of adventures new.
8. An 1828 song cycle by Schubert concerning a recently dumped young man's journey of desperation that ends in his death.
9. A state that this proposed journey to the vanishing point aspires to.
10. Were the travelling point to ever arrive at the vanishing point, its velocity would be infinite.
11. The numbering system allows for the fact that the point is travelling in the opposite direction from the racing shells.
12. From the 'Technical Manifesto of Futurist Painting' by Umberto Boccioni, Carlo Carra, Luigi Russolo, Giacomo Balla and Gino Severini, initiated in 1909 by FT Marinetti in the pages of *Le Figaro* newspaper. The Manifesto was launched on 18 March 1910 in the limelight of the Chiarella Theatre of Turin – see www.italianfuturism.org/manifestos/futuristpaintersmanifesto/. Either this enigmatic dictum suggests a supposedly joyous interchange of awareness between the bus passengers and the residents of the adjacent houses who, provoked by the

200-decibel din of the oncoming bus, conjure the engine with its fiery pistons pumping in and out; and, in turn, the passengers, seeing the houses flash by, imagine the lives lived therein. Or that some sort of actual physical blending takes place, albeit temporary. Being of a literal bent of mind, I hope it is the latter; for such an interpretation allows that the Futurists thought of the 'drive-in house' back in 1910.
13. From the oft-quoted article by Reyner Banham: 'A Home Is Not a House', first published in *Art in America*, April 1965, p 3. The title is a play on words. Polly Adler, described as a notorious madam, had previously written a book recounting her experiences entitled *A House Is Not a Home*: Polly Adler, *A House Is Not a Home*, Rinehart & Co (New York and Toronto), 1953. I realise I have just added to the verity of the 'oft-quoted' remark by one.
14. James Howard Kunstler, *The Geography of Nowhere*, Simon & Schuster/Free Press (New York), 1994.
15. A method of describing the surface of an object derived from ship hull design.
16. From the text version of a lecture I delivered at the University of Waterloo, Canada, in 1973.

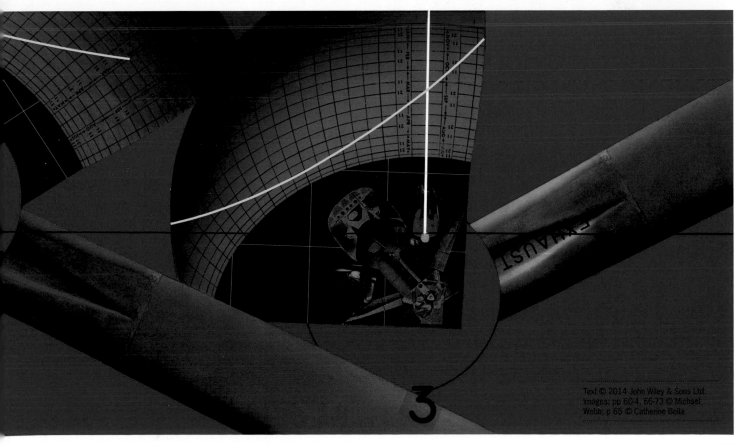

Ralph Parker/Price & Myers
Geometrics, Slipstream, Terminal 2,
Heathrow Airport, 2013

Ralph Parker and Tim Lucas

TRIPPING THE FLIGHT FANTASTIC

SLIPSTREAM
TERMINAL 2
HEATHROW AIRPORT

Ralph Parker and Tim Lucas of
Price & Myers Geometrics explain
the complex architectural and
engineering challenges of turning
a simple idea – solidifying the
motion of a joyfully cartwheeling
aircraft – into a vast kit-of-parts
jigsaw puzzle for Richard Wilson's
new sculpture at Heathrow.

Artists and architects have long concerned
themselves with motion. In the early part of the
last century, the Futurist Umberto Boccioni's
bronze sculpture *Unique Forms of Continuity in
Space* (1913) imagined the strange volumes
carved in air by the dynamic motion of the
body. At a similar time, for quite different
reasons, Eadweard Muybridge and Frank
Gilbreth corralled photography to expand
motion beyond human perception.

Today, computing power is in some senses
catching up with Boccioni's future dream. For
Slipstream – a Richard Wilson sculpture in
the new Terminal 2 at Heathrow – the artist
imagined an aircraft on a fantastic acrobatic
trajectory through the space, and architect
Ralph Parker devised from first principles a
method of designing and capturing the motion
of the aircraft, before processing the result into
a 76-metre (249-foot) jigsaw kit of over 30,000
unique parts. Echoing construction techniques
from the aerospace industry, each of the
22 cassettes that comprise the sculpture
are built on a production-line assembly from
individually CNC-labelled interlocking, self-
setting-out pieces. Sophisticated engineering,
involving wind tunnel and blast testing, allows
the 70-tonne sculpture to span between four
pre-existing columns flying 20 metres (66 feet)
above the concourse.

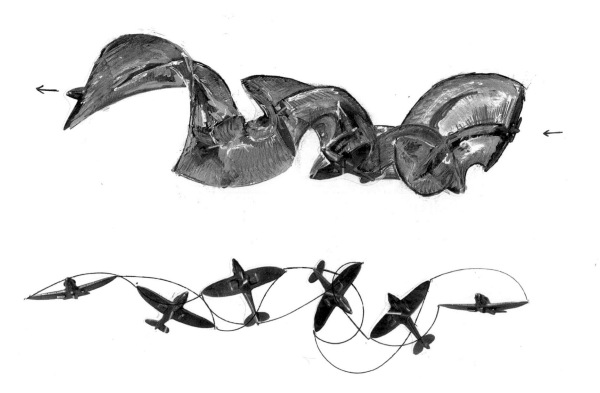

Ralph Parker/Price & Myers Geometrics, *Slipstream,*
Terminal 2, Heathrow Airport, 2013
Computer-generated image of the half a million
programmatically generated rivet positions on the sculpture.

In mathematical terms, to calculate precisely the 'shape in space' described by a complex volume (a hand, or an aircraft) as it moves on a non-linear path is extremely challenging, indeed arguably impossible without some level of discretisation; for example, simplification of the source object, or its trajectory. Swept volume algorithms (for piston heads, undercarriages etc) tend to use a level of discretisation of the trajectory, usually to create a 'mesh' representing the swept envelope. They, like Muybridge's picture series, capture discrete moments in time: a subtle distinction, but a greatly simpler prospect than representing the entirety of the motion. Gilbreth's long-exposure photographs manage to capture this entirety, albeit projected onto the effectively two-dimensional plane of a photographic plate. What was required for *Slipstream* was an approach that worked as Gilbreth's plates had, but in three dimensions.

Besides these esoteric differences, other important considerations included design, structural action and buildability. The motion had to be authored by the artist and the architect, while fitting within the envelope of what was structurally viable as calculated by the Price & Myers' team of engineers. Time and procurement dictated that the form be constructed using only panel-based, CNC-cut parts – a 'flatpack' sculpture, simple and quick to assemble. A mesh-based approach would not be sufficient here, thus calling for a particular type of surface construction: ruled and developable. The architectural challenge of creating this unique form, and translating it into a buildable kit-of-parts for rapid assembly, required a novel combination of film animation software, aerospace design tools and scripting to accomplish.

Beginning with film animation software, the motion of the plane was designed inside the building information model (BIM) of the terminal building. Careful attention was paid to creating an elegant, continuous trajectory; almost 50 iterations were honed before the final movement, satisfying structural and aesthetic demands, was found. Smooth motion, logically, gave rise to a more harmonious (and easier to fabricate) form. The completed animation consists of 300 frames, similar to 300 Muybridge-like 'snapshots' of the motion, only in three dimensions. Using a series of scripts to process the large datasets involved, the trace of each vertex in the aircraft over the course of the 300 frames was formed into a spline describing its motion. The splines were then 'Gilbreth-ed' – joined by the script in sequence to create a series of ruled, developable, continuous ribbon surfaces.

The generation of the sculpture from the source motion is rational, but the resulting form, though beautiful, in construction terms is highly irrational. By comparison the form of an aircraft is predicated by function, and usually largely symmetrical; however each point on the *Slipstream* sculpture differed, often markedly, from every other. Nevertheless, drawing on the language and software of the aerospace industry, it was possible to develop an integrated model of more than 30,000 unique pieces, generated by parametric modelling together with complex custom scripts, running many millions of operations.

**Price & Myers Geometrics, *Slipstream*,
Terminal 2, Heathrow Airport, 2013**
Exploded view of a typical unit showing
steel armature, plywood ribs, bulkheads and
skins, and aluminium cladding.

Due to its length – equivalent to a Jumbo
Jet – and in order to segue with the main
contractor's sequencing, the sculpture was
split into 22 cassettes that were manufactured
off site. The size of each cassette was
dictated by what could be transported on a
standard low-loader truck. A custom script
calculated the minimum bounding box
dimensions of each cassette.

Construction began with the 76-metre
(249-foot) steel skeleton, onto which were
attached a series of 110 OSB bulkheads –
effectively vertical slices through the sculpture
– threaded like jigsaw pieces around the
steelwork. Linking these together are a series
of plywood spars, or 'combs' – so called
because of their notches and edges where
they form leading and trailing extremities
– which set out the complex surface of the
sculpture. A dual layer of thinner, curved ply
forms the continuous skin of the sculpture;
each panel is dovetailed into its neighbours,
and has CNC pre-drilled holes corresponding
to the edges, combs and bulkheads below to
ensure accurate alignment. Onto the upper
layer of ply is scribed the setting-out pattern
for the aluminium panels, effectively printing
the sculpture's instructions upon its surface.
Each piece of OSB, plywood and aluminium
has a unique ID that is written onto its surface
via CNC. Generating the sweeping lines of
rivets that delineate the movement through
space of vertices on the aircraft's surface
involved the creation of over half a million
points in space, each with a its own unique ID.

Scripts were used to generate the plywood
skin components and the aluminium panels,
adding the dovetails and pre-drilled holes to
the former, and the rivet cut-outs to the latter.
In addition, where the generated pieces were
larger than standard sheet sizes, the script
added dovetailed splices and calculated the
optimum placement of the piece on a sheet
to minimise wastage. These complex scripts
needed to deal with input pieces that displayed
a high degree of variance in shape and size,
and several million unique operations were
required to generate the complete set.

Construction began with the 76-metre
(249-foot) steel skeleton, onto which were
attached a series of 110 OSB bulkheads
– effectively vertical slices through the
sculpture – threaded like jigsaw pieces
around the steelwork. Linking these
together are a series of plywood spars, or
'combs' – so called because of their notches
and edges where they form leading and
trailing extremities – which set out the
complex surface of the sculpture.

A Rhythm In Four Dimensions

In a warehouse on the outskirts of Hull, the strange hulks of cassettes are aligned, in various states of completion. Several are bare steelwork; skeletons awaiting the timber flesh and aluminium skin that will make them corporeal. Further along the assembly line, timber frames are in evidence. The bulkheads echo with the shape of the aircraft, abstracted by motion. Seams of dovetail joints allow the steel tubes to pass through them. Notches in the comb and edge spars slot into corresponding notches across the bulkheads. This ensures that one corner of each comb touches the outer skin layer; a continuous line of setting out for the subsequent two layers of plywood deck. Accuracy established by the combs allows CNC-drilled holes in the first ply layer to line through and fix into them. Where pieces are larger than a standard-sized sheet, dovetail joints split the panel. The construction is intelligent, low cost and beautiful.

At the far end of the workshop, the twisting volumes are clad in aluminium. Some of the ribbons of metal strips are shallow, others curved tight, thin, intricate. The planes' motion is revealed as a complex four-dimensional form: the pattern of rivets illustrates the passage of time – closely spaced where the speed is low, spreading apart where the aircraft moves fast.

Structuring the Slipstream

There are generally two approaches to the structural design of a sculpture: add strength to a weak or brittle material with an internal armature, or use the strength of the sculpture's material to make it structural in itself. The scale and complexity of *Slipstream* demanded the internal structure approach. The armature weighs 35 tonnes and is 76 metres (249 feet) long, and enables the sculpture to be supported at four points, 18 metres (59 feet) apart.

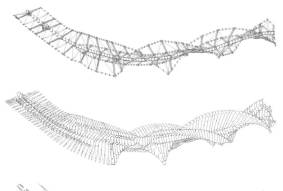

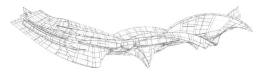

Views showing separated component types.

Trial erection of three units in Hull.

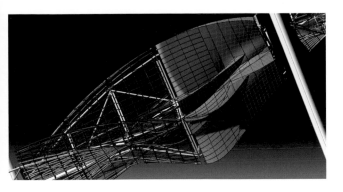

View of Catia model showing the steel structure under the plywood and aluminium skin.

The envelope of a building usually has plenty of space for a structure; for example, with a bridge the size and form of the structure informs the visual design. For *Slipstream* it was necessary to undergo a three-way iterative design process of controlling the form via the plane's flight path, understanding the volume created, and checking that a structure of adequate strength could fit inside. It took 48 versions to arrive at a form with a structure that could be accommodated.

Structural engineering is fundamentally about creating load paths between any part of a building and the ground. For *Slipstream*, a structurally sound load path has to link any part of the sculpture and the ground. The load path starts from the outer aluminium skin and continues through a plywood stressed skin, into plywood ribs, through OSB bulkheads and into the central steel armature. From here the load passes along the steel armature – formed from 22 bolted truss sections spanning like a contorted bridge through the sculpture's volume – to supporting bearings fixed on the steel columns that hold up the roof of the terminal building, and finally down into the ground. The challenge of creating a structure where each element is unique in shape was solved by developing a system of structural joints between each element in the load-path hierarchy that essentially does the same job. Materials are screwed, slotted, tied and bolted together in such a way that the geometry will always fit within these structural connections.

Material choice is based on both structural and fabrication considerations. The fabrication principle was to assemble notionally two-dimensional plywood and OSB parts into a complex three-dimensional shape. Flat timber panels were fundamental to allowing the unique shapes to be cut. For the armature, steel is the only material that has the strength, stiffness and adaptability to fit within the sculpture's skin and allow it to be manoeuvred and lifted easily. In common with the other elements in the sculpture, the steel armature is standardised but customisable. Divided into 22 similar but different units, the structure weaves and undulates through the volume. It is based on a central 400-millimetre (16-inch) steel box section core, with arms at either end that extend towards the surface of the sculpture. Steel bracing tubes join the arms to each other and back to the core. This simple system, joined with bolted 20-millimetre (0.8-inch) thick steel plates, gives the sculpture strength and crucially connects to all the bulkheads. The strong steel core allows each unit of the sculpture to be lifted, moved and erected without affecting the plywood and aluminium.

With installation of the sculpture underway, over three years of prototypical research and development, testing and construction are entering their final phase. Encompassing art, architecture, engineering and construction, *Slipstream* is a novel addition to that pantheon of works reflecting on the ephemeral tracks man leaves while moving through his world. ⌂

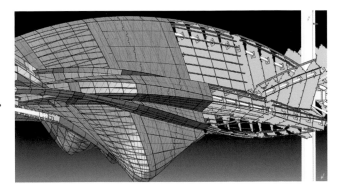

View of Catia model showing the aluminium and plywood skins over the bulkheads.

Tobias Nolte and Andrew Witt

GEHRY PARTNERS' FONDATION LOUIS VUITTON

CROWDSOURCING EMBEDDED INTELLIGENCE

The complexity of the mass-customised forms of Gehry Partners' new art museum in Paris, the Fondation Louis Vuitton pour la création, has taken high-definition simulation techniques and embedded intelligence to a new level. **Tobias Nolte and Andrew Witt** of Gehry Technologies describe how the realisation of the Fondation required the development of a 3D concurrent design system that could synchronise hundreds of participants. This self-optimisation system has enabled both 'intricate collaboration and unprecedented engineering'. The benefits have been far reaching, ranging from the detailing of tolerances to material constraints.

Gehry Partners LLP, Fondation Louis Vuitton pour la création, Paris, due for completion early 2014
Installation of the tertiary structure of the glass envelope. The glulam beams that form the primary structure are protected by a black covering.

The project is remarkable for the geometric complexity of the design, the scope of collaboration, and the progressive attitude of the client. All these factors combined created the perfect environment for innovation around process to manage both geometric and organisational complexity.

LVMH.

F.GEHRY APR. 06

High-precision design tools are quickly moving from the merely analytic and generative to the more simulational, and near real-time optimisations provide the promise of reactive feedback of unprecedented richness. Digital models become repositories not merely of geometry, but of conceptual and material rules for building simulation that interact immediately with the designer's intent. The laws of material itself can reciprocally inform design gestures, creating a truly synthetic process in which the architect orchestrates all aspects of the project with computational accuracy.

Beyond simulated rules of design, project execution requires the collaboration among a spectrum of disciplines, each with specific technical and resulting geometric intentions, rules and logics. This simultaneous digital definition of distinct dimensions of the project by designers, engineers and builders could be called concurrent design. Rules of customisation, deformation, fabrication and assembly are dynamically proposed and tested in a single, intelligent, self-documenting model.

A project that has taken the notion of embedded intelligence – and self-optimising simulation rules – quite far is the Fondation Louis Vuitton pour la création, a major new museum for contemporary art in Paris designed by Frank Gehry. The Fondation will host a permanent collection, rotating exhibitions, performances and lectures. Situated in the Bois de Boulogne just outside the *périphérique* to the west of Paris, the project breaks dramatically from traditional geometric and material principles by mass-customising folded glass and curved concrete panels on a huge scale. The envelope is an alternation of 19,000 fibre-cement panels and 3,500 curved-glass facade elements, each different and parametrically optimised for its specific local geometry. The design, engineering, construction and fabrication includes several high-profile collaborators, including Studios Architecture (executive architects), RFR/TESS (facade engineers), Setec Bâtiment (structural and mechanical engineers), Vinci (general contractor), Eiffage Construction Métallique (facade contractor), Hofmeister Roofing (facade contractor), Sunglass (fabricator) and Bonna Sabla (fabricator). The ground was broken in 2009 and it is currently under construction, with completion planned for early 2014.

The project is remarkable for the geometric complexity of the design, the scope of collaboration, and the progressive attitude of the client. All these factors combined created the perfect environment for innovation around process to manage both geometric and organisational complexity.

Implicit Material Optimisations

The major design challenge of the Fondation was to mass-customise glass and concrete panels to specific curvatures on an unprecedented scale. Take, for instance, the curved-glass facade. To achieve this effect, the fabricator, Sunglass, used a large parametric glass mould that allowed the precise bending of glass sheets into cylindrical geometry. Of course the contours of the design surfaces were in fact freeform, or at best developable – a far cry from the strict geometry of the cylinder. Gehry Technologies developed tools to find the best-fit cylinder for each of 3,500 freeform shapes – fitting these 1 x 3 metre (3.3 x 9.8 foot) cylinders to within 5 millimetres (0.2 inches) of the design surface. This required the embedding of fabrication and geometry rules in the model itself, including optimisations – a new step in embedded generative intelligence and simulation.

In the past, generative methods have been largely used for design explorations, often assuming that implicit geometry or a very few rules of thumb suffice for validating design feasibility. But in fact the mechanical processes of fabrication often have decisive impacts on the design geometry itself, particularly at the detail level. Validation on this level often requires dozens of parameters to be analysed for each assembly piece, even

for apparently simple systems. Systems intended for design exploration alone are not sufficiently robust, reliable or simply extensible to give the detailed feedback required in these situations.

For the Fondation Louis Vuitton, Gehry Technologies consultants worked directly with project engineers to create intelligent reusable modules to validate details automatically and generatively. Over 200 reusable detail components were designed in collaboration with the engineers, notably RFR/TESS, for the design validation and quantities control of hundreds of custom conditions. Since these modules, like the rest of the model, were stored on a model server, the engineers could modify their details with full technical knowledge while other team members could still validate the pure spatial aspects of the designed details. The generation of these details, after the design of the initial prototype, was distributed across many machines, courtesy of the cloud model server.

The centralisation and redistribution of the model facilitated a new scale of design computation and optimisation, which ultimately was necessary to address some of the complex geometric issues of the project. Since many analyses and generative exercises for the building were computation

above: Workers install the glass-reinforced concrete Ductal panels and the transportable panel unit (TPU) substrates on the southwest facade of the building. Each Ductal panel is individually moulded, and the larger TPUs on which they are fixed are composed of built-up layers of steel, insulation and waterproofing.

below: View of the virtual model of all glass cylinders visualising particular design parameters in a colour range.

Process map of the automation steps to generate
the documentation of the glass-reinforced concrete
Ductal panels.

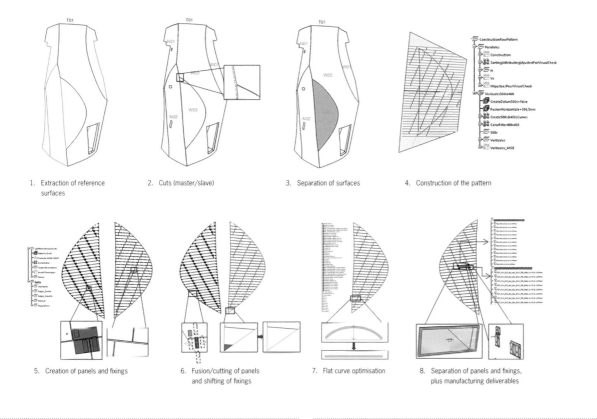

1. Extraction of reference surfaces
2. Cuts (master/slave)
3. Separation of surfaces
4. Construction of the pattern
5. Creation of panels and fixings
6. Fusion/cutting of panels and shifting of fixings
7. Flat curve optimisation
8. Separation of panels and fixings, plus manufacturing deliverables

intensive and time consuming, an early initiative of the team implementing collaboration practices was to facilitate the offloading of this processing to other machines, or to low-demand machines. Essentially, a private cloud for generative geometry and optimisation was created, specifically to find the material deformations that would best fit the ambitious global design. This capacity was leveraged to generatively detail the most complex parts of the building.

In addition to the use of the concurrent design systems to validate hundreds of custom details, the cloud provided a natural way to scale-up computation methods for design optimisation. Methods more often used for statistical analysis – curve fitting, least squares fit and similar procedures – were embedded within the model to implicitly optimise its geometry.

By having a model distributed through the model server, several computers could simultaneously optimise separate portions of the project in a concurrent and independent way. The generality of the approach proved to be remarkably versatile, moving well beyond typical surface constructability problems to the computation of minimum mould sizes and fitting of optimal structural fixing plates. The project demonstrates the broad promise of these new implicit methods, and the possibility of deploying radically more general

and powerful methods of surface analysis and optimisation for architectural constructability. It also points up the power of serving a model on the cloud, where sophisticated calculations can be batched out on demand.

The advent of the concurrent design system as a method of distributed optimisation pointed the way to other automatic uses of the centralised data, leading to the implementation of some task-specific servers, such as clash reporting, routine file conversion, and data extraction, which continue to evolve as the project proceeds.

Crowdsourcing High Precision
Precision is all well and good among experts, but what happens when models with embedded intelligence are scaled up to project teams? Besides the geometric complexity, the Fondation Louis Vuitton project also faced an organisational complexity rooted in its globally distributed nature. The design architects are in Los Angeles, while most of the design teams are in offices in Paris. There were various other participants on both the design and construction side in the UK, Germany, Belgium, Spain and Italy. In all there were over a dozen companies involved in the design and construction process, all of whom needed some level of access to current 3D information.

*Paris's new formal landmark will
not only be a marvellous new use
of materials, but a bold new way of
organising the design enterprise itself.*

Many of these teams needed to define certain aspects of the geometry parametrically in the same model. The goal was to overcome a traditional, linear planning process in favour of a more integrated, concurrent design approach across designers, engineers, builder and fabricators.

Real ways to build integrated models are urgent needs in today's design world. Building systems are far too complex for single players to master, and the digital model provides a way to make these system rules accessible elsewhere. Systems that share digital models seamlessly can provide benefits such as accelerated distribution of information, more direct accountability, simpler reporting, and automatic and batch processing of complex computations on dedicated servers.

The Fondation required a 3D concurrent design system for not dozens, but hundreds of participants. There was no tool that came close to what was necessary – so Gehry Technologies built one.

Initially, the tool was built on Subversion (SVN), an open-source versioning and locking system more commonly used for source code in large software projects. In fact, software development and buildings share a great deal: both have many contributors, with mutual dependencies, on tight schedules, often geographically distributed. The best ideas from software development were therefore taken and applied to architecture. SVN enabled movement of the model to the cloud, and combining the polyglot model base – Digital Project, XSteel, SketchUp, Rhino, and many other platforms – into a common resource for over 400 designers, engineers and builders. From this first effort, Gehry Technologies went further to create GTeam, the world's most advanced multi-platform building information model (BIM) navigator for Web and mobile. GTeam combines social computing, accountability, data visualisation/mining and approval cycle workflow into a single high-precision assembly tool, a true means to crowdsourcing high-accuracy design.

As the Fondation Louis Vuitton speeds towards completion, its challenges, achievements and lessons have been folded back into the knowledge culture of Gehry Technologies. Perhaps most significantly, the project was a high-performance test case for how embedded intelligence can activate and enable intricate collaboration and unprecedented engineering. Self-optimising systems can execute on rules as diverse as detailing tolerances and material constraints. Paris's new formal landmark will not only be a marvellous new use of materials, but a bold new way of organising the design enterprise itself. ⌂

top: Night view of the installation of a major element of the secondary structure, which will support one of the large glass canopy surfaces above the building.

bottom: View of the north facade, with several of the major canopies already having fully installed glass.

DIFFUSIVE THERMAL ARCHITECTURE

Philip Beesley

Philippe Baylaucq, Stills from
***ORA*, 2011**
opposite: Dancers were recorded using high-definition stereoscopic thermography. An expanded physiology of traces leading into surrounding surfaces of floors and walls was revealed.

Philippe Baylaucq and Philip Beesley, Hylozoic Series, 2013
bottom left: Breathing frond covering head. Varying levels of thermal energy generated by the author's internal metabolism are visible through polymer membrane surfaces.

bottom right: Detail of head and hand holding polymer frond. A heat trail is visible leading from the author's hand.

NEW WORK FROM THE HYLOZOIC SERIES

Philippe Baylaucq and Philip Beesley, Hylozoic Series, 2013
Exhaled carbon dioxide. Precisely calibrated thermal imaging shows cycling waves of thermal energy from exhaled carbon dioxide moving through the core of a frond mechanism.

Could the use of high-resolution image equipment and the thermodynamic patterns that they produce have a significant application in architectural design? Architect **Philip Beesley**, a professor at the School of Architecture at the University of Waterloo in Canada, describes the explorations revealed by the Hylozoic Series, a collaborative series of immersive architectural environments directed by a team from the university. He explains how the subtle effects of the works are achieved by integrating active filters into canopies and screens that create immersive, forest-like installations.

From within an immersive suspended canopy made from laser-cut filter frond components, an occupant reaches out and touches its surface. A thermal image of this gesture captures every bundled muscle fibre within the subject's face and neck. The bridge of his nose and his eyes glow white while the cooler tips of his nose and ears recede into darkness. The palm of his hand radiates heat, coursing upwards through the outstretched tips of the fingers that touch the prototype frond details. The hand is giving to the inanimate material, and at the same time the frond is pulling heat out from the body, feeding itself. A stream of warmth leads upwards from the material adjacent to his uppermost fingertips. Delicate tapered Mylar branches standing close to the fingers glow, a trail of contact that flows up their lengths while it dies away into the cool surround. Within a second image from the same series using a smoke chamber, trembling tines extend out from each leaf-like filter frond, sweeping through the humidity-laden plume that wafts along the outer surface. The slowly pulsing current is cupped and concentrated by the arcing motion, making a spiralling pool that gathers close to the base of the frond's spine. When the surface sweeps down, the pool releases and shifts into an arcing sweep of opposing spirals, current and crosscurrent alternating. A darkened laminar plume of clear air along the lee of the upper frond surface is opened. Tendrils follow the clearing with accelerating rebounds, sending a necklace of miniature spirals back towards the surface.

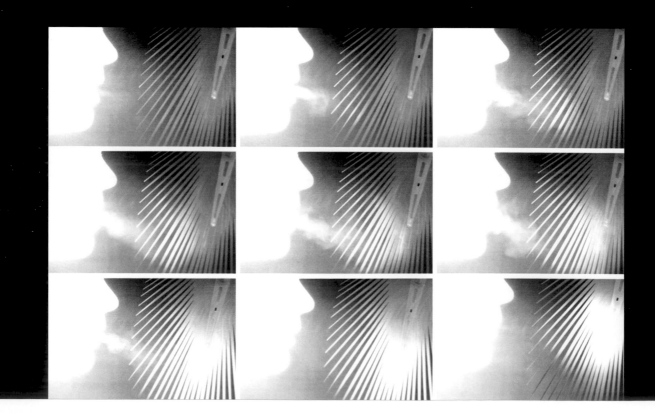

These suggestive images are born from the design process of emerging components from the Hylozoic Series, a collaborative series of immersive architectural environments led by a team from the University of Waterloo School of Architecture, Cambridge, Ontario. The new generation of this work focuses on subtle phenomena. Details from the emerging work show a preoccupation with intimate human touch interacting with extremely lightweight materials diffusing into the surrounding air. Thin layers of voided hovering filters are tuned for delicate kinetic and chemical responses that cohere as expanded physiologies, while beckoning and sharing space with viewers.

The work presents a state of quiet, setting out ghost-like crystalline forms following diagrids and textile forms that make lightweight, resonant scaffolds. Nested clusters of infrared proximity sensor arrays support a densely interwoven network that allows viewers and component systems to communicate in tribal clusters. Increments of gentle muscular movements within the physical components register viewer presence, rippling back to offer a sense of a breathing, ambient architecture. When occupant activity heightens, the structures of this space can become saturated with turbulence that offers clutching and pulling, imparting a fertile churn. The form-languages of this work seek radical involvement with the immediate perimeter as well as the broader world. This might imply equations that are quite distinct from the Vitruvian conceptions that have prioritised enclosing territory and maximum defensiveness, and have seemed to dominate Western architecture. By encouraging maximum possible involvement and by offering fragility and resonance, the work offers efflorescent involvement and exchange.

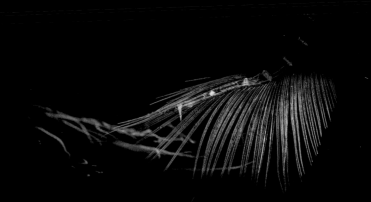

Philip Beesley and collaborators, Breathing Frond Smoke-Chamber Test series, Hylozoic Series, The Leonardo, Salt Lake City, Utah, 2013
top: Trails of smoke reveal convection patterns moving through the laser-cut tines of a Hylozoic series breathing frond mechanism.

Philip Beesley, Breathing Frond Smoke-Chamber Test series, Hylozoic Series, 2013
bottom: Convection plumes are revealed by the cycling of a shape-memory alloy frond mechanism.

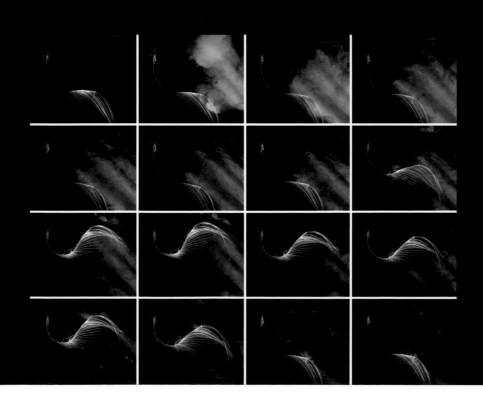

Philippe Baylaucq, Stills from ORA, 2011
Arrayed dancers – high-definition stereo thermal cinematography. Varying patterns of thermal energy from inner metabolisms of dancers are vivid in this production still. Cool layers of insulating outer tissues show dark, masking light-appearing inner anatomy with striking individual variations.

opposite: Thermal imprint with liquid nitrogen erasure – high-definition stereo thermal cinematography. Liquid nitrogen is visible as radiating dark trails erasing the bright imprint of a dancer's body on the stage floor of the *ORA* production set. Nitrogen is used for flash erasure of heat traces, clearing the stage in preparation for new recording.

Air, Gas, Fluids

Could the emerging thermodynamic patterns within the physical fragments described in these passages suggest a practical design for new architecture? Technical crafts present a design space where air, gas and fluids can be manipulated as building materials. The Yale mechanical engineer Michelle Addington suggests how energy exchanges around the body and around buildings can be addressed in exchanges that expose the pervasive dynamic of convective plumes around all physical objects within the atmosphere.[1] High-resolution imaging equipment can be tuned to detect movements of energy embodied within component systems and flowing through the gaseous and liquid environment that surrounds them. If pressure and heat differentials could be controlled, their boundaries could become a primary building 'material' for building envelopes.

The Hylozoic Series has integrated active filters into canopies and screens that make immersive, forest-like environments. These diffusive systems include protocells and synthetic cells, organised by fluxing gradients of alternating aqueous chemical concentrations, suspended within viscous fluids that form sheltering beds for delicate formations. These 'Lisegang ring' formations imply the first stages of skin and structure formation, condensing in gradients akin to the layered densities of rainbows. Condensing fluids are housed within masses of acrylic plates that run through microprocessor-controlled suspended canopy and wall surfaces, a kind of fluid circulation system that could one day work like lymph and blood within a building enclosure capable of breathing and thinking.

Thermography Reveals Subtle Dimensions

Design methods for this work shown here combine late 19th-century imaging techniques for photography of kinetics, 20th-century wind-tunnel and fluid dynamics, and contemporary high-resolution sensing. High-resolution helium-cooled thermal cameras such as those first used by the Quebec filmmaker and Hylozoic Series collaborator Philippe Baylaucq are emerging as tools for designers. The images shown here employ mid-wave infrared thermal photography, with an indium antimonide detector that can be tuned to read wavelengths from 1,000 to 5,000 nanometres, instead of the 450–750 nanometre range of sensors used for photography of visible light. Typical thermography reveals form by filtering out the atmosphere. Baylaucq's cinematography goes further, however, implying an expanded range that includes interactions between wall, floor and ceiling surfaces and their occupants.

In a scene from Baylaucq's 2012 high-resolution three-dimensional thermal film entitled *ORA*, a braided wreath of bodies reaches around in an open tribal circle. José Navas's choreographed gestures create murmuring ripples between the intertwined dancers, while the surface that supports the circle echoes with their traces. Shifting in a spiral, each dancer slowly rolls and turns while the print of their skin remains embedded within the floor. The camera creates a poignantly intimate space, where every part of their bodies glows in detail – darkened cool breasts, nose and chin; white-hot abdomen, throat and eyes. The floor tracings carry the same anatomy, glowing small of back and abdomen pulled into the floor, while the shapes of colder buttocks and shoulder blades leave masked and darkened shadows. A continual eroding wake spreads behind as the circle shifts.

Baylaucq and the author are now working together, developing a three-dimensional thermal film entitled *Sylva* that extends a dialogue that emerged during the *Sibyl* project of 2012. The title's Latin definition evokes primordial forests and might serve as an origin-myth for contemporary architecture. Early studies for the film are included here. In one image, a frond filter is positioned to hang vertically as a semi-conductive thermal screen. It partly masks the glowing face looking straight towards the camera. In the spaces between the narrow, tapering tines of the frond, the facial structure is etched as a map that betrays the knotted bundles and fibrous clusters lying below the smooth profiles of the jaw and throat. The cool tip of the nose is partly covered by the converging stem that gathers the frond's tines at its centre. The stem follows the shadow, fading to dark, while above at the pineal gland and bridge of the nose it glows white-hot. Lingering in the surface of the frond is a shifting map of facial energy.

Typical thermography reveals form by filtering out the atmosphere. Baylaucq's cinematography goes further, however, implying an expanded range that includes interactions between wall, floor and ceiling surfaces and their occupants.

If 'notch' filters applied to thermal detectors are tuned to precisely address gaseous material, minute air currents and concentrations of carbon dioxide and oxygen can be seen concentrating and dispersing around our bodies, extending in laminar flows along inner and outer surfaces of building envelopes. Demonstrating a coarse example, a second series of images uses schematic tuning to reveal breath from a viewer passing over a filter frond. The thin tips of the frond quickly absorb the energy of the breath, passing it into the thickened centre of the filter which is fed by the dense surround of multiple tines. There is a tangible sense of living and inorganic exchange in these images. After the warming breath ceases, the heated centre moves upwards into the stem, while the outer tips of the frond quickly reverse their flow and darken, pulling cold from the surround.[2]

In parallel with the work emerging with Baylaucq, a new collaboration with the Amsterdam-based haute couture designer Iris van Herpen is underway. The work follows a conception of vestment that extends from the surface of the body, extending tendrils and plumes outwards, interweaving with the layers of air that surround human bodies. Van Herpen's Voltage series, presented at a 2013 Paris Fashion Week event, increases the sensitivity and delicacy of individual components derived from architectural screens, transcending into ethereal, expressive clothing. Clusters of laser-cut translucent Mylar fronds are arranged by moulaging their angled geometries around an inner sheath that closely fits the body. Cantilevered resilient stays are inserted, permitting outward extension that creates a halo-like cloud of hovering material rippling and vibrating in response to bodily gestures. In a second fabric type, a robust silicone meshwork swarms around the body. Individual impact-resistant acrylic chevron links are chained together with small silicone tubes to form a diagrid of corrugated mesh with diffusive, viscous performance.

Diffusive Form-Language

The intimate dimensions implied by collaborations with Baylaucq and Van Herpen imply form-languages for designing urban buildings. If architects follow the Vitruvian tradition that has guided centuries of North American and European building designs, we will continue to see trim, clean, stripped surfaces and dense, crystalline forms – pure cubes, rectangles and domes. These forms make a kind of language that hearkens back to the Greek philosopher Plato, who described the world as coming from an inner core of pure geometry. There are good reasons, however, to pursue the opposite of these kinds of stripped forms. Instead of valuing resistance and closure, design for thermal exchange could result in new form-languages based on maximum interaction. If designs are configured for uncertain conditions where acquiring and shedding heat play in uneven cycles, then the kind of diffusive form-language seen in reticulated snowflakes, heat sinks and the microscopic manifolds of mitochondria offer an alternate optimum. These examples have a common form-language of radical exfoliation. Their increased surface areas can make their reaction surfaces potent. Writ large, these forms speak of involvement with the world. Indeed, the systems that appear within life-giving forests and jungles are opposite to abstract cubes and spheres. The densely layered forms of a jungle are often made of diffusive, deeply interwoven material that expands and interacts with its surroundings. A new city built to be able to easily handle unstable conditions where it could shed heat, cool itself and then rapidly warm up and gain heat again might well look like a hybrid forest, where each building is made from dense layers of ivy-like filters and multiple overlapping layers of porous openings.

Iris van Herpen, Voltage haute couture, 2013
opposite: The studios of Van Herpen and Philip Beesley collaborated in developing diffusive frond fabrics used for the Voltage series, presented in Paris in January 2013.

Philip Beesley, *Sibyl*, Hylozoic Series, Sydney Biennale, Australia, 2012
Sibyl integrates next-generation details from the Hylozoic series including massed ventilating bladders, scent-glands, and vibrating fields of filter mechanisms.

A building system using an expanded range of reticulated screens and canopies is implied, constructed from minutely balanced filtering layers that can amplify and guide convective currents encircling internal spaces. Within this vanguard city fabric, the thermal plumes emitted by each human occupant offer a new form of energy that could be ingested, diffused and celebrated.

Reticulated Grottos

Influenced by these explorations, new architectural installations within the Hylozoic Series offer dense reticulated grottos. Fissured valves are clustered around carbon dioxide-laden air intakes within a new series of component clusters within the *Radiant Soil* installation, positioned as the portal to Paris's 'En Vie, aux frontières du design' exhibition at l'Espace Fondation EDF. The porous valves serve carbon-capturing 'Leduc cells', a chemical reaction that converts dissolved carbon dioxide into harmless carbonates, much like chalk or limestone. The jaws of these valves are counterbalanced, configured to stir and gently pump air through their surfaces when they are stirred by the slight air movements brought by visitors moving through the environment.

A suspended layer of organic batteries is positioned as an adjacent reticulum, providing weak intermittent pulsing that in turn triggers rolling waves of LED light from helical chains of fluid-filled glass chains. Akin to unconscious breathing or intermittent tidal movements, this series of triggers provides internal cycling that works in parallel to other external sensor impulses provided by the reactions of occupants. The assembled warren of glass chains is wired to function with overlays of behaviour, creating an extremely primitive 'brain' cluster that remembers traces of past pulses in the form of subsiding overlapping echoes.

The installation *Epiphyte Cloud* features new structural systems related to the suspended works seen within *Radiant Soil*. In a prototype architectural textile canopy installed at a series of venues throughout France, including Maubeuge, Lille and Créteil, radial free-form slitting patterns are arranged within discs of stainless steel and impact-resistant acrylic. Tulip-shaped hyperbolic spars are formed through thermoforming and mechanical expansion of these laser-cut planar units. Interlinking spars are organised in a hexagonal tile-work that creates a strong, resilient reticulum capable of carrying substantial loads. A foam-like structure is organised from multiple layers of this component system and carries dense masses of fluid-filled glass vessels.

Rather than the historical humanist conception in which architecture functions as a stable surface supporting free human action, a stripped and stable horizon, the architecture that could result from this work offers a soil-like, hovering meniscus. Such a surface might offer fertile involvement that requires mutual relationships and negotiation with the surrounding environment. This implies a renewed kind of stewardship of our environment. Rather than insisting on enclosing territory and maximum defence, the forms shown here seem to seek expansion and diffusion within their perimeters. Guided by an alternate optimum to the durability and stability preferred by Vitruvius, this architecture pursues the maximum possible involvement and minimum defence, seeking instead an efflorescence of involvement and exchange.

This range of processes tend to be characterised by delicacy, resonance and resilience. If my clothing floats and ripples outwards, and if fluxing heat and cold cloaks me, then it might not be necessary to say that the boundaries of my body lie at my skin, and that the boundaries of a building are defined by an enclosing envelope. Instead, conception of buildings can increasingly move from older ideas of a static world of closed boundaries towards the expanded physiology and dynamic form of a metabolism. ∆

Notes
1. 'A human body walking through a room will create numerous shifts in conditions: the temperature difference between the human skin and the surrounding air will produce an exchange of heat between the body and the air; moving air will affect the humidity immediately adjacent to the body … As long as the human body is alive and present, the various energy exchanges will occur … boundaries are constantly emerging, mutating, and dissolving.' See Michelle Addington, 'Architecture of Contingency', in Philip Beesley (ed), *Hylozoic Ground: Liminal Responsive Architecture*, Riverside Architectural Press (Cambridge, Ontario, 2010), p 71.
2. Thermal imaging reproduced in this article was produced with the generous assistance of Arne Adams/IRCameras and Austin Richards/FLIR.

Rather than the historical humanist conception in which architecture functions as a stable surface supporting free human action, a stripped and stable horizon, the architecture that could result from this work offers a soil-like, hovering meniscus.

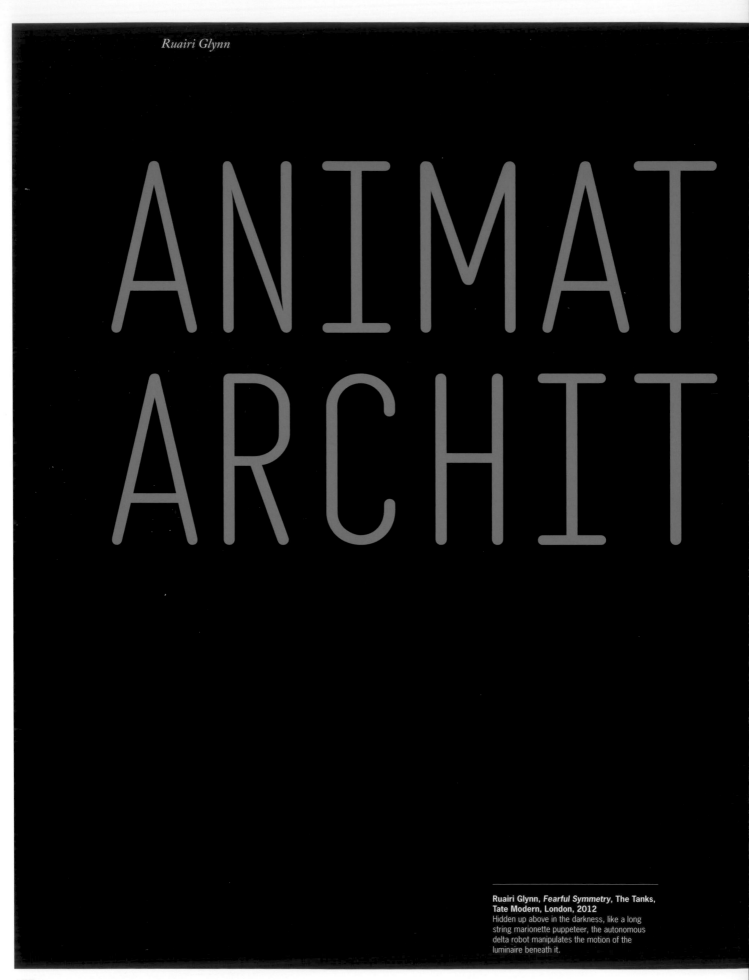

Ruairi Glynn

ANIMAT
ARCHIT

**Ruairi Glynn, *Fearful Symmetry*, The Tanks,
Tate Modern, London, 2012**
Hidden up above in the darkness, like a long
string marionette puppeteer, the autonomous
delta robot manipulates the motion of the
luminaire beneath it.

ING
ECTURE

Ruairi Glynn, lecturer on interactive architecture at the Bartlett School of Architecture, University College London (UCL), puts the pressing question: 'What does a world of hyper-connective, high-definition sensing offer architectural design?' Despite the pervasiveness of ubiquitous computing – the Internet of Things (IoT) – and students' ability to speculate, build and test responsive life-size installations, could practice itself be in danger of getting left behind?

COUPLING HIGH-DEFINITION SENSING WITH HIGH-DEFINITION ACTUATION

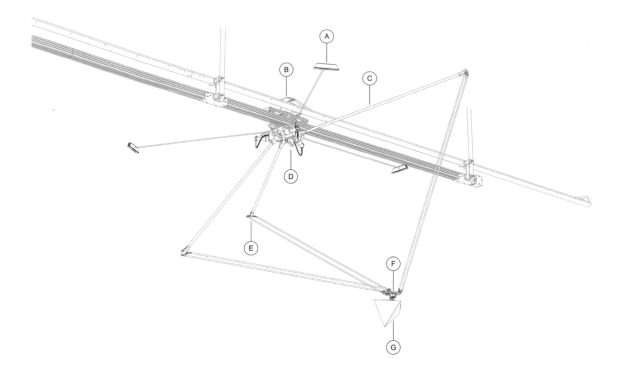

Annotated illustration of the 5-metre (16-foot) tall custom-built delta robot: (a) Kinect sensor array; (b) 21-metre (69-foot) linear carriage; (c) carbon-fibre structure; (d) central robotics platform; (e) parallel mechanism; (f) pan and tilt servomotors; (g) electroluminescent tetrahedron.

Harnessing live sensor feeds, social media, maps, and a deluge of datasets gathered by networked devices and distant servers, context-aware computing is changing our means of engagement and occupation of the city. But this appears to be just the tip of an iceberg. Internet-enabled devices are bifurcating, promising to do to our buildings what they have done to our cities. Virtually every corner of product and service design is investing itself in ubiquitous computing, the Internet of Things (IoT) (see Andrew Hudson-Smith's article on pp 40–47) – call it what you will. If it lives up to its evangelists' promises, we should expect embedded sensing and computing to saturate our homes and workplaces. Billions of active devices building dense, rich layers of real-time sensor data where even our own clothes may monitor our biodata to share with the 'cloud'. These vast datasets, latent with novel applications for consumers and industry alike, beg the question: What does a world of hyper-connective, high-definition sensing offer architectural design?

Looking to today's schools of architecture you find, with surprising abundance, students literate in Internet protocols and scripting, hacking together electronics, and programming microcontrollers. What started in a few experimental studios has spread globally, catalysed by the open-source hardware revolution. Affordable and accessible technologies are encouraging students not only to speculate, but to build and test responsive installations at 1:1 scale. Ecological and conversational models of communication and adaptation are pushing design thinking beyond reactive paradigms and towards truly interactive environments. After decades of speculation and prototyping within academia, the technologies to practically realise sensor-rich buildings capable of adapting to inhabitant activity, responsive to individual needs and surrounding conditions are becoming accessible. The path to their broader adoption, however, is far from clear.

Looking to practice, the response to the emerging IoT has been cautiously slow. While the building industry might acknowledge its potential to change the built environment profoundly, it has resisted taking a leading role in its arrival. As William Gibson once remarked: 'The future is already here – it's just not evenly distributed.'[1] And from all early indications, it is consumer markets that will build this smart infrastructure – architects and building engineers will be largely bypassed while they continue to follow established holistic approaches to so-called 'smart' or 'intelligent' buildings.

Rendered view looking up. A central robotics platform actuates three carbon-fibre armatures that descend down to collaboratively puppeteer its end effector – a glowing electroluminescent tetrahedron that appears to float in the air while the robot hides in the darkness above.

Ruairi Glynn, *Fearful Symmetry* out of the shadows, London, 2012
Ruairi Glynn walks by his custom-built machine at his Walthamstow workshop, revealing the scale of the world's largest delta robot.

Elaborating on the age-old thermostat model, current approaches incorporate sensing, computation and actuation within the fabric of the building. For a variety of reasons, not least, mitigating risk, holistic approaches are generally based on closed proprietary systems – good at dealing with well-defined domains such as room temperature or light levels, but not so good at dealing with unpredictable domains like human behaviour, changes in programme and in surrounding climatic, social and economic conditions. Over the lifespan of a building, this inflexibility ultimately results in human control being either constrained or an illusion altogether.[2]

IoT offers a very different approach principally built on open-source protocols. Sensor networks, built ad hoc, are flexible regarding relocation and replacement – growing over time as cost, accessibility and services improve and expand. As ubiquitous sensing and computation gradually infiltrate, building data densifies and diversifies. Machine learning algorithms running on remote servers collect and make sense of these complex interconnections, feeding back into the environment through available local actuation. As these open connective platforms grow, designers and communities develop new applications. The result – a dense, self-organising computational field permeating material and spatial practices, from textile, product and service design to furniture, landscape and architecture.

These two approaches to building responsive architecture are worlds apart. The holistic top-down model, rigid and reductive but complete and predictable. The IoT bottom-up model, intangible and bewildering to many, but adaptable and extendable. One trend emerging in the automation industry is a turn towards open-source hardware platforms as they prove their robustness. This may well offer the convergence point between these approaches. Of course predicting future technology adoption can be perilous for even the best-informed observer, but if, as IoT evangelists suggest, sensor networks get built and distributed informally over time, with distant servers making sense of the growing datasets, then sensing and computation will have been largely lifted from the responsibility of the architect and building engineer. The key role remaining in this scenario will be to 'close the loop' – designing the forms of actuation that feed back into the built environment.

With the diversity of actuation technologies expanding almost as fast as sensing, a fertile territory is opening up. As robotic applications for the built environment bifurcate, space is becoming increasingly motive – from fine-scale, micro-actuated composite materials to

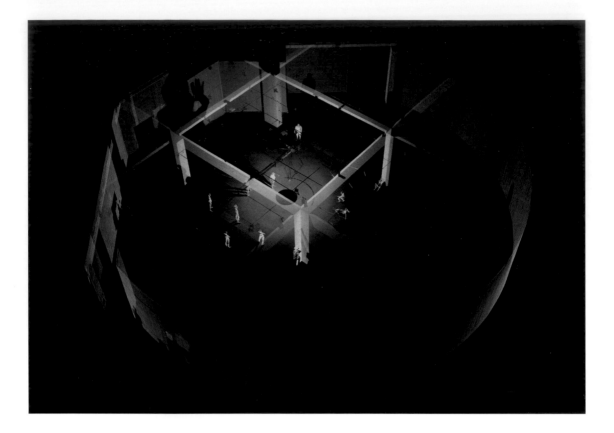

adaptive building facades; from autonomous ground and air vehicles to all forms of virtual agency in augmented-reality landscapes. As the resolution with which buildings detect and interpret human behaviour increases, we can anticipate sophisticated reciprocal gestures from our built environment as delicate and deliberate as those made by its inhabitants. Through the coupling of high-definition sensing and actuation, space will become ever more animate, perceptively possessing a life of its own, populated with agency, in constant conversation with its surroundings.

Fearful Symmetry

Exploring the perception of life or 'anima' in form and space, _Fearful Symmetry_ was commissioned by Tate Modern for the 'Undercurrent' programme inaugurating its new 'live art' space, the Tanks.[3] The cavernous concrete chamber of the south tank, 32 metres (105 feet) in diameter and 7 metres (23 feet) tall, had previously lain dormant for decades, cloaked in darkness. The response to the site was a living luminaire revealing the dramatic space as it moved around the gallery interacting with the visiting public. Primitive in appearance, to avoid figuratively inferring life, a piercing glowing tetrahedron glided through the air, swooping down to play with visitors and fleeing up and away if too

many got close. Taking its title from William Blake's 'The Tyger',[4] the installation intended to create a visceral state of hyper-awareness in the public as they encountered the intimidating dark chamber and the strange life-form that inhabited it.

Hidden up above in the darkness, like a long string marionette puppeteer, a 5-metre (16-foot) tall autonomous delta robot, custom built to manipulate the motion of the luminaire beneath it, moved back and forth through the space on a 21-metre (69-foot) motorised rail. An array of Kinect sensors mounted on the travelling robot built a real-time 3D point cloud of its local environment, detecting the public and reading their individual movements using gesture-recognition algorithms. Reciprocally, the agile performer responded with behaviours choreographed with the collaboration of a team of puppeteers, giving the machine its uncannily human character.

Encouraging the public to suspend their disbelief and play with the living luminaire, the more people engaged gesturally with the work, the more enthusiastic its responses would be. If visitors were stationary it would hover over them, slowly turning mechanically and abstractly, almost mocking their inanimateness. With the subtlest change from mechanical to smooth fluid motion, the

Through the coupling of high-definition sensing and actuation, space will become ever more animate, perceptively possessing a life of its own, populated with agency, in constant conversation with its surroundings.

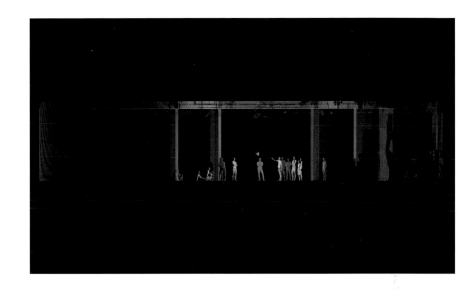

work transformed from a lifeless platonic solid to a living breathing performer. Precise motion control of the delta robot manipulator was critical, but far more important was creating the perception that the movements were purposeful. With sophisticated analysis of the public's gestures, the autonomous robot reciprocated with a perceptible intelligence and emotion. While at first intimidating to visitors of the Tanks, many of the public became increasingly comfortable and confident in performing with their luminous companion as their exchanges developed.

Two decades ago at the dawn of the World Wide Web, Kevin Kelly proclaimed that:

The central act of the coming era is to connect everything to everything. All matter, big and small, will be linked into vast webs of networks at many levels. Without grand meshes there is no life, intelligence, and evolution; with networks there are all of these and more.[5]

Today, the Internet of Things appears to be at the dawn of its realisation. Will we find ourselves two decades from now sharing a built environment teeming in animate forms of intelligence and synthetic life? While contemporary architectural research in robotics has focused on its potential for digital fabrication applications, there is another rich territory of interaction that deserves greater attention – one offering architects exciting opportunities to build aesthetically potent environments[6] that will profoundly change our relationship and engagement with architecture. ∆

Notes
1. William Gibson, quoted in *The Economist*, 4 December 2003.
2. Jared Sandberg, 'Employees Only Think They Control Thermostat', *Wall Street Journal*, 15 January 2003: http://online.wsj.com/article/SB1042577628591401304.html.
3. The design and fabrication of *Fearful Symmetry* was made possible with the generous support of the Bartlett School of Architecture, University College London (UCL), the department of Product Design Engineering, Middlesex University, and the Centre for Robotics Research, King's College London: see www.fsymmetry.com/.
4. Published as part of Blake's collection of poems, *Songs of Innocence and Experience*, 1794. Tate Publishing; Facsimile edition, 2 October 2006, p 40.
5. Kevin Kelly, *Out of Control: The New Biology of Machines*, Perseus Books (New York), 1994, p 173.
6. Gordon Pask, 'A Comment, a Case History and a Plan', in Jasia Reichardt (ed), *Cybernetics, Art and Ideas*, Studio Vista (London), 1971, pp 76–99. In the article Pask discusses the properties of aesthetically potent environments, 'of environments designed to encourage or foster the type of interaction which is (by hypothesis) pleasurable'.

IMPOSSIBLE OBJECTS

Jonathan Proto and Brandon Kruysman of Kruysman-Proto, both design technologists at San Francisco-based Bot & Dolly, a design and engineering studio that specialises in automation, robotics and filmmaking, describe their radical approach to architectural representation. They explain how by combining cinematic techniques and advanced robotic manufacturing they have been able to explore a new model for making that shifts the role of robotics in fabrication away from a process largely focused on geometric rationalisation into the sphere of visualisation and ideas creation.

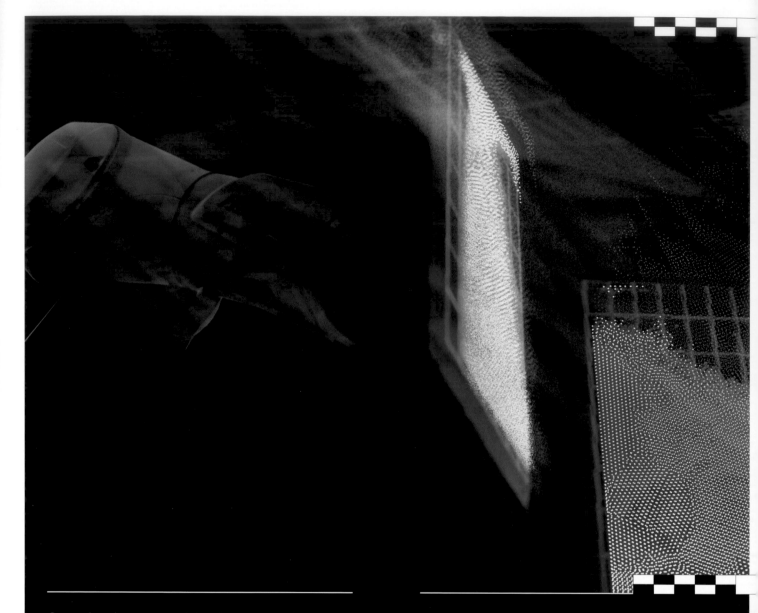

Our media culture is primarily based on images and accessed through screens. The screen has become the mediator through which we experience things; nothing is meant to be experienced in depth, but explored instantaneously on a two-dimensional surface.[1] By combining robotic motion control with animation techniques, the two-dimensional flatness of the screen is challenged, opening up new potentials in image-making that extend beyond the flat screen into hybrid realities where the production of representation and the representation itself become blurred. This research centres on the development of an animation-based robot motion control platform to push the boundaries of the 'screen', where virtual objects are no longer constrained to the space of the frame, but start to interact with physical space. The platform was developed by Kruysman-Proto in 2011 during a Fellowship at the Southern California Institute of Architecture (SCI-Arc), and utilises both a time- and event-based approach to multi-robot motion control.

In the 'Eye, Robot' experiment for a seminar of the same name led by Kruysman-Proto at SCI-Arc, long-exposure photography in combination with robotic motion control was

Kruysman-Proto, Projection Mapping on Moving Objects, Los Angeles, 2012
A real-time system was developed by Kruysman-Proto to projection-map onto moving objects. Live visuals based on particle simulations are updated in real time based on actual robotic motion.

Kruysman-Proto, Chandelier Prototype 01, Los Angeles, 2013
opposite: Match-moving in combination with compositing techniques allows for virtual prototyping in digital fabrication scenarios, overlaying both virtual and physical objects through the precise calibration of cameras. In this experiment for a chandelier prototype, different robotic cell configurations and end-of-arm tooling versions could first be tested virtually.

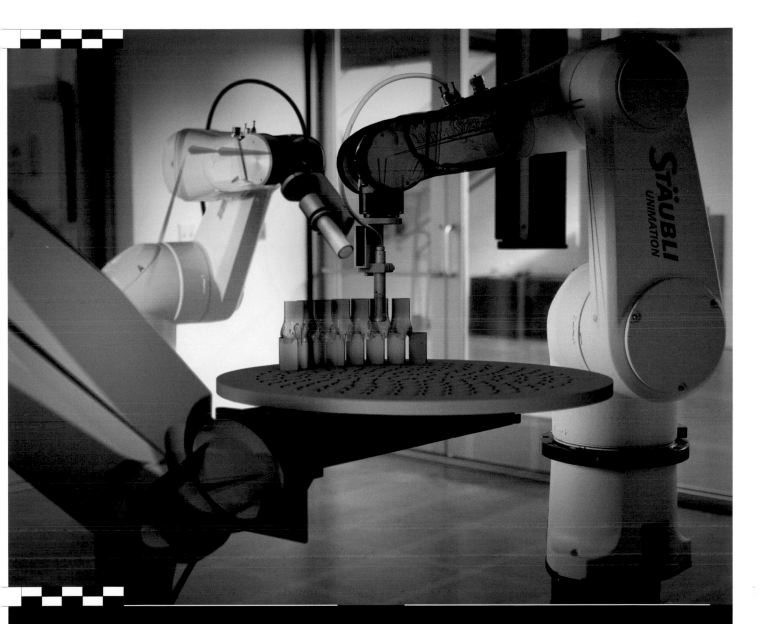

pushed to its limits. The project focused on the tracking and precise positioning of objects in space using synchronised robots, programmable cameras, as well as moving images on a large screen. Influenced by bullet-time photography and virtual cinematography techniques, the experiments used a combination of animation and automation to suspend an object in motion with programmable cameras. Using a plasma television playing a 60,000-frame long-section cut animation, the robot pulls the movie through space while synchronised to the shutters of digital single-lens reflex (DSLR) cameras controlled by robots. The resulting short movie stitches together hundreds of photographs, each 10-second-long exposures. This work challenges the notion of the screen, and subjects the visualisation to the physical constraints of space.

The custom animation-based robotics platform has provided a unique understanding of the translation between architectural representation and production. Through a time-based approach to motion control using very precise feedback

algorithms, a model for robotics has been created that opens up new possibilities for architectural representation, speculation and visualisation, with the ability to both combine and juxtapose virtual and physical worlds. In this interface, objects are not just one directional; virtual objects are not simply translated into the physical world, but rather exist in a non-linear exchange between both. For example, the translation from the virtual world to the physical world (or the reverse) exists in a loop, where simulation starts to look more like material, and the physical world is becoming more virtual. These types of exchanges begin with the assumption that although the gap between representation and reality can never be completely bridged, it is getting closer than ever before seen with robotics. Kruysman-Proto's The Net and Projection Mapping on Moving Objects experiments both aimed to blur this boundary further. Using software-based physics engines usually employed primarily to approximate physical systems, the studies aimed to do just the reverse and apply virtual dynamics and forces to physical robotic arms,

challenging the notion of simulation and approximating virtual systems in actual space.

Match-moving and compositing techniques have changed the way in which we think fundamentally about boundaries and the contents of a location. Green screening and match-moving allow spaces to no longer be constrained by geographic location, but rather defined by other variables related to high-precision robotic motion control and compositing techniques. This type of digital workflow, although unbound by the physical constraints of space, is defined primarily by another variable – time.

The production of these composite image sequences requires a precise understanding of time, and in Kruysman-Proto's case the primary unit of measurement is referred to as the 'keyframe'. Precision is not just defined by the position of an object in space, but the precision of that object in motion over time. Conceptually, this extends to synchronisation strategies where each individual object in the robotic cell has its own timeframe. A custom communication protocol

was developed in order to have a global time clock that is constantly adjusting in real time through 'cueing', just as in choreographic systems. In this sense, synchronisation is both event based and time based, which allows for a communication system for multi-robot scenarios that can react to disruptions and alterations in the actual environment.

Combined match-moving and simulation concepts have led to advancements in the speculation of advanced manufacturing through virtual prototyping. These types of architectural prototypes are not purely physical things, but augmented objects that exhibit both virtual and physical characteristics in the formulation of a concept, before its actualisation.[2]

The synchronisation of images on external screens with actual robotic motion requires real-time compositing techniques. Beyond just a traditional image or animation, the virtual prototype is confronted with the physical constraints of space, engaging both machinic and environmental factors such as acceleration and velocity, as well as issues of scale.

The resulting image does not operate simply as an analogue for something beyond itself, but is also the thing itself.[3] It is materially and technologically mediated through the use of high-precision robots and a custom animation platform.

This approach to architectural representation is generative: on one hand scientific, and on the other purely visual and speculative. These types of images move beyond thinking about representation as a model; they act as the model and the thing itself. In Kruysman-Proto's Chandelier Prototype Number 1, simulation and material studies were done in parallel, resulting in a project that extends beyond the images or videos themselves, or the physical prototype itself.

The combination of both cinematic technique and advanced robotic manufacturing explores a new model for making that shifts the role of robotics in fabrication as a process of geometry rationalisation into producing new ideas of how designers make things and visualise ideas. ∆

Kruysman-Proto, Chandelier Prototype 02: Material Testing, Los Angeles, 2013
opposite: Initial studies of the chandelier prototype, testing heat fusing and material deformation.

Kruysman-Proto, Chandelier Prototype 03: Material Testing, Los Angeles, 2013
opposite inset: Detail of chandelier prototype heat-fused joint.

Kruysman-Proto, Augmented Fabrication, Los Angeles, 2013
Kruysman-Proto developed a real-time overlay system using an external screen in combination with calibrated cameras, showing path procedure, patterning strategy and the virtual end-of-arm tool prototype composited onto live footage with an actual robot.

Notes
1. Matthew Fielder, '*On the Accuracy of Fiction*', *The Real-Fake*, p 2: www. real-fake.org/pdf/fieldertext.html.
2. Barbara Bolt, *Art Beyond Representation: The Performative Power of the Image*, IB Tauris (London), 2004, p 18.
3. Ibid, p 16.

Richard Beckett and Sarat Babu

TO THE MICRON

A NEW ARCHITECTURE THROUGH HIGH-RESOLUTION MULTI-SCALAR DESIGN AND MANUFACTURING

Richard Beckett (DMC London), Sarat Babu (Betatype) and Vasilis Chlorokostas, Interface /4, Bartlett School of Architecture, University College London (UCL), 2013
opposite: Details of the front membrane under rear lighting shows both the surface texturing and material translucency. The majority of the construct is 1 millimetre (0.04 inches) thick.

Richard Beckett (DMC London) and Sarat Babu (Betatype), *Cilia*, SCIN Gallery, London, 2012
below: Surface tiles featuring fibrous protrusions with varying lengths between 20 and 100 millimetres (0.8 and 3.9 inches) and varying thickness between 0.5 millimetres and 2 millimetres (0.02 and 0.08 inches). Each tile is constructed as a single piece with a density of approximately 100 fibres per centimetre.

Richard Beckett (DMC London), Sarat Babu (Betatype) and Alexandrina Rizova, Fragile, Covent Garden, London, 2012
bottom: Sculpture resulting from a structural investigation into minimal material application across complex volumes. The piece sits within a volume of 0.3 square metres (3.2 square feet) using less than 1 kilogramme (2.2 pounds) of material.

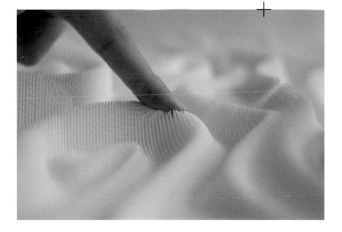

Rapidly shrinking tolerances and increasing fidelity of emerging additive layer systems are beginning to afford a new opportunity: the ability to design below the macroscopic scale. This is resulting in the engineering of hybrid materials in which every element of their properties can be prescribed at the point of design conception. **Richard Beckett** of the Digital Manufacturing Centre (DMC), London, and the Bartlett School of Architecture, UCL, and **Sarat Babu** of Betatype explore a potential new architecture that encompasses a scalar hierarchy of matter, enabling design to take place concurrently at scales ranging from the micrometre to the metre.

If material is considered through a hierarchy of structure, the act of designing synthetic materials is one of enforcing control over these structures at various dimensional scales to exhibit properties of our choosing.

Design, then, is the shaping of material at the macroscopic scale through form. Its evolution has been influenced directly by the advancement of our methods of form representation. Computation has provided the most radical shift in our methods of prescribing volume – a toolset that abstracts form to a dimensionless yet absolute state. Limitations in what can be rendered are no longer defined by the complexity of the representation but rather our ability to understand the language of formal construction, to translate contextual inputs into the representation, and render the representation at zero tolerance.

Additive-based methods of construction offer perhaps the most direct route of physically rendering forms shaped by digital tools. Their limitations as a construction process, however, have been due to the physical qualities of the resulting objects.

Selective laser sintering is one of a number of commercial processes that begin to encroach on the realm of traditional manufacturing. Here the sintering of polymer powders enables the production of materials with comparable properties to engineering-grade plastics. At the same time, the unique feature of the process produces stable structures with wall thickness as fine as 400 micrometres.

Richard Beckett (DMC London), Sarat Babu (Betatype) and Vasilis Chlorokostas, Interface /4, Bartlett School of Architecture, University College London (UCL), 2013
top: Detail of the front surface under a natural backlight.

bottom: Detail of the rear membrane showing mesostructural elements of the construct.

At these dimensions, we begin to blur the boundaries between form and material. The use of additive fabrication methods to build hybrid materials is not new,[1] but what is novel is the ability to adapt design tools to include both macroscopic form and material properties, to fabricate them on current commercial additive manufacturing systems, and engage in localised control of material properties throughout their physical volume.

Exploring the use of selective laser sintering (SLS) has been the core focus of a research collaboration between Betatype and DMC London, working to understand the practical limits, capabilities and properties that can be exhibited through a persistent material dataset created by digital and physical testing.

Such a potential for complete control is both liberating and paralysing – freeform high-definition fabrication requires an equally high-definition design context. Designing in this space not only requires new methods and tools; there is also a need to relate back to function through human interaction.

*Such a potential for complete control
is both liberating and paralysing –
freeform high-definition fabrication
requires an equally high-definition
design context.*

Note
1. Emanuel Sachs, Michael Cima, James
Cornie, David Brancazio, Jim Bredt, Alain
Curodeau, Tailin Fan, Satbir Khanuja, Alan
Lauder, John Lee and Steve Michaels,
'Three-Dimensional Printing: The Physics and
Implications of Additive Manufacturing', *CIRP
Annals – Manufacturing Technology*, 42(1),
1993, pp 257–60.

Interface /4 is one iteration in an ongoing series of experiments that attempt to converge upon a vision for architecture through practice. Exploring the notion of a high-definition interface, the 1:1-scale prototype explores a design concurrently at the scales of micron to metre, adapting mesoscopic structures to illicit optical details while maintaining a bulk structural stiffness-to-weight ratio that enables practical application within its spatial boundary. The approach enables a huge amount of flexibility in response to a site context without the need for the gross volume of the shape to change; rather, the context of the envelope can be adapted to respond through a broad range of optical and mechanical properties. Future iterations will expand upon the physical properties that can be adapted, including thermal and electrical types, in order to control a far broader range of dynamic capabilities.

The Interface experiments are by no means a prescriptive take on what this architecture might be, but an attempt to explore the physical reality of a new language for architecture that matches the potential of additive manufacturing. ᴆ

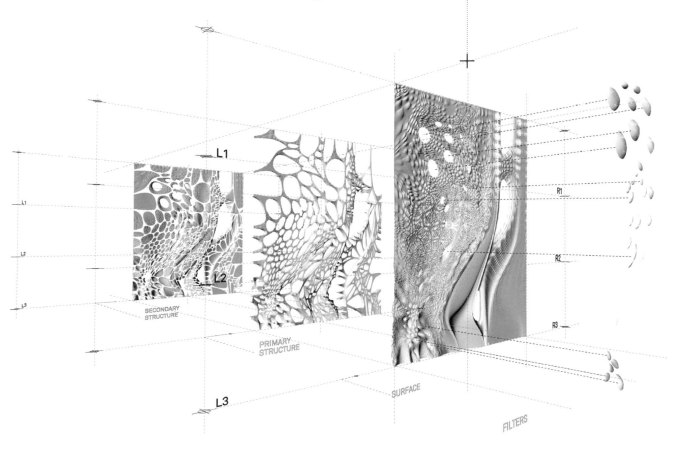

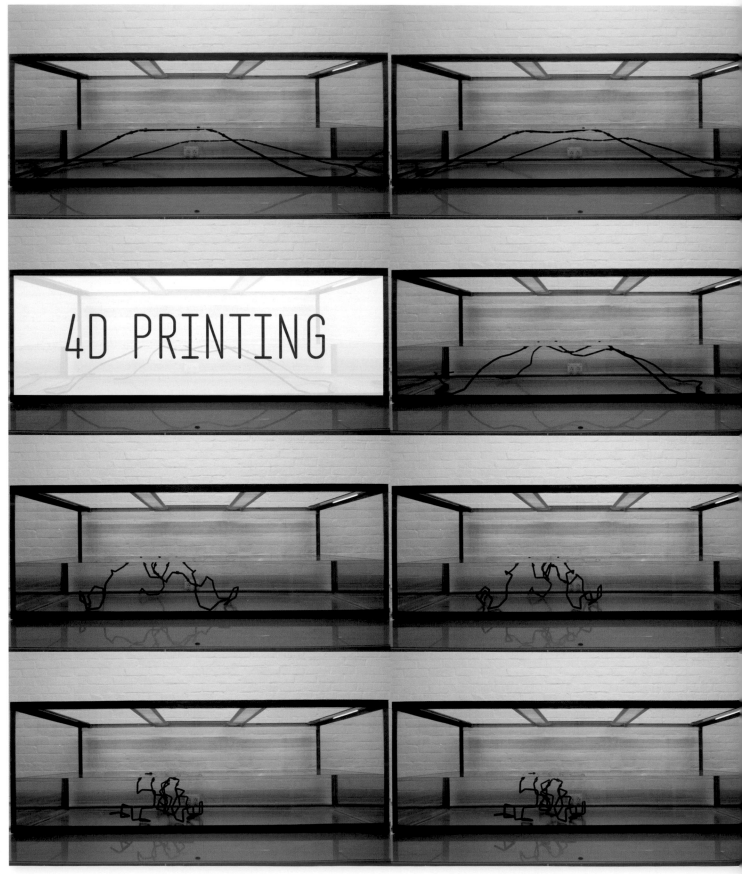

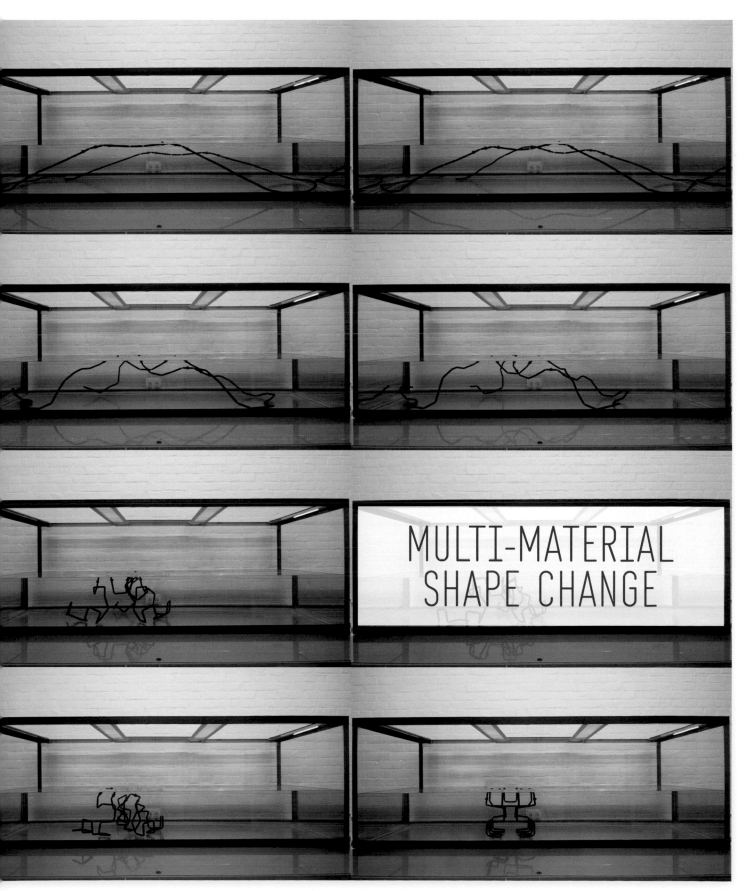

MIT Self-Assembly Lab and Stratasys (Skylar Tibbits, Shelly Linor, Daniel Dikovsky and Shai Hirsch), 4D Printing, 2013
Self-folding of a 4.3-metre (14-foot) long 4D-Printed multi-material single strand into a second-generation Hilbert cube.

MULTI-MATERIAL SHAPE CHANGE

How might 4D printing overcome the obstacles that are hampering the rolling out and scaling up of 3D printing? **Skylar Tibbits,** Director of the Self-Assembly Lab at the Massachusetts Institute of Technology (MIT), describes how the Lab has partnered up with Stratasys Ltd, an industry leader in the development of 4D Printing, and is making the development of self-assembly programmable materials and adaptive technologies for industrial application in building design and construction its focus.

Additive manufacturing and rapid prototyping have developed at exceptional rates and gained wide acceptance since their invention in 1984 by Charles Hull. Also the founder of 3D Systems, Charles Hull invented stereolithography as a new process for viewing and testing designs before investing in full production.[1] Today, these technologies are used in countless industries, in the home and across the globe. The ability to mass-produce customised components without substantial increases in time, material or inefficiency has been coined as one of the revolutionary advantages of additive manufacturing. However, the realities of our current capabilities are far behind our expectations and visions for additive manufacturing technologies. Further, mass-customisation ignores the time and energy needed after custom parts have been printed, requiring excessive sorting and labour-intensive assembly.

Some of the main applications for printing today include food, toys and proof-of-concept prototypes, thus falling far short of our visions for revolutionising manufacturing.[2] At the 2013 US Manufacturing Competitiveness Initiative Dialogue on Additive Manufacturing, Boeing's Michael Hayes highlighted this issue by outlining the main hurdles that lie ahead for additive manufacturing, including: a larger build-envelope and increased scale for printing applications; structural materials that can be used in functional and high-performance settings; and multi-functional and smart/responsive materials.[3]

Each of these hurdles will need to be addressed and likely combined in order to truly demonstrate the scalability of additive manufacturing to rival existing manufacturing efficiencies. The Self-Assembly Lab at the Massachusetts Institute of Technology (MIT) has as its focus the development of self-assembly, programmable materials and adaptive technologies for industrial applications in the built environment. These phenomena are viewed by the Lab as one of the most important processes in both natural and synthetic systems, and a principle that crosses nearly every discipline, offering a new opportunity for making smarter materials and better techniques for construction. A number of self-assembling, self-reconfiguring and programmable material prototypes have therefore been developed, emphasising the scalability of such principles across materials, fabrication technologies and external energy sources.[4] However, many of these prototypes have required an additional production step of embedding 'programmability' and the potential energy for transformation; for example, magnets, elastic strands, Nitinol wires, rachetting mechanisms and many others. This challenge, of streamlining the process of production for programmable and adaptive materials, has led to the collaboration with Stratasys Ltd, an industry leader in multi-material printing, and the development of 4D Printing, aimed at offering streamlined multifunctional printed material systems.[5]

4D Printing

4D Printing is a new process that demonstrates a radical shift in additive manufacturing. It entails multi-material prints with the capability to transform over time, or a customised material system that can change from one shape to another, directly off the print bed. This technique offers a streamlined path from idea to reality with performance-driven functionality built directly into the materials. The fourth dimension is described here as the transformation over time, emphasising that printed structures are no longer simply static, dead objects; rather, they are programmably active and can transform independently.

With Connex printing capabilities and 4D Printed materials, a single print, with multi-material features, can transform any one-dimensional strand into a three-dimensional shape, any two-dimensional surface into a three-dimensional shape, or morph from one three-dimensional shape into another. Using only water as its activation energy, this demonstrates a new possibility for production and manufacturing. Similarly, adaptive and dynamic responses for structures and products are now plausible without adding time, cost or extra components to make systems 'smarter'. As environmental, economic, human and other constraints continue to fluctuate, we will continue to require highly resilient systems that can respond with ease and agility. 4D Printing is a first glimpse into the world of evolvable materials that can respond to user needs or environmental changes.

At the core of this technology are three key capabilities: the machine, the material and the geometric 'programme'. Stratasys's Connex machine offers multi-material PolyJet printing with a variety of material properties from rigid to soft plastics and transparent materials, and high-resolution control over dot deposition. The dynamic material was developed with the Stratasys material research group and is a hydrophilic polymer that expands 150 per cent when it encounters water. The printer deposits a rigid polymer material simultaneously with the expanding 'active' material to give both structure and potential energy. The final component important for the viability of 4D Printing is the design and placement of the geometric programme that embeds the capability for state-change directly into the materials themselves.

The rigid material gives the structure and angle limiters for folding. When the part is printed it has an initial position, then after encountering water the active material swells, forcing the rigid material to bend. When the rigid material hits neighbouring elements, it is forced to stop folding and thus has reached the final-state configuration. The placement and volume of the rigid and active materials encompasses an embedded geometric programme and the activation energy to transform from one shape to another, completely independently.

MIT and Stratasys have developed a variety of physical prototypes, including strands that fold into the letters 'MIT' and complex self-folding Hilbert curves, each demonstrating transformation from one-dimensional and two-dimensional flexible shapes into rigid structures.

The first structure was printed as a single strand roughly 30 centimetres (1 foot) in length, containing both rigid and active materials. When dipped in water, the single strand transforms into the letters 'MIT', demonstrating a 1D to 2D shape-change. The second experiment also utilised a single strand; however, this 46-centimetre (18-inch) strand, when submerged in water, transformed into a rigid wireframe 3D cube. At each of the joints, two rigid discs were printed that acted as angle limiters, which when folded and touching one another forced the strand to stop at 90-degree angles. Geometrically, this cube is the first generation of a fractal Hilbert curve, where a single line is drawn through all eight points of the cube without overlapping or intersecting. Second- and third-generation Hilbert curves, measuring approximately 4.3 metres (14 feet) and 15 metres (50 feet) in length respectively, were also generated and self-folded, with each folding into a 20-centimetre (8-inch) Hilbert cube.

A second series of structures demonstrate surface transformations. In this case, a two-dimensional flat plane was printed, with both rigid and active materials. This flat plane represents the six unfolded surfaces of a cube. At each of the joints a long strip of active and rigid materials was printed that describes a 90-degree angle limiter that stops the surface from folding when it reaches the final-state condition. When submerged in water, the surface folds into a closed-surface cube with filleted edges. A wide range of other 1D, 2D and 3D transformations are also possible including self-folding origami, self-healing structures where holes close after encountering water, and other global geometric reconfigurations.

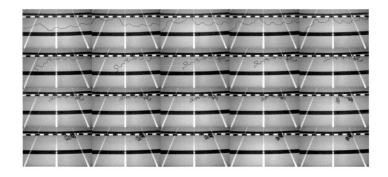

MIT Self-Assembly Lab and Autodesk Research (Skylar
Tibbits and Carlos Olguin), Project Cyborg, 2013
Project Cyborg software simulation of a 4D-Printed single
strand folding into a three-dimensional cube.

New Physical/Digital Toolsets

In order to take advantage of this new transformational technology, from initial idea to physical reality, MIT has collaborated with Autodesk Research in its development of a new software package. Project Cyborg is a design platform spanning applications from the nano scale to the human scale. The software offers simulation for self-assembly and programmable materials as well as optimisation for design constraints and joint folding. The aim is to tightly couple this new cross-disciplinary and cross-scalar design tool with the real-world material transformation of 4D Printing. The coupled software and hardware tools will eliminate the traditional paradigms of simulating then building, or building then adjusting the simulation. This workflow aims to create simulations that adjust physical performance and materials that promote new simulated possibilities, offering top-down and bottom-up evolution of design possibilities both physically and digitally.

Future Applications

The Self-Assembly Lab's vision for the future of products and processes has radically shifted with the introduction of programmable printed materials. Personal and responsive products will adapt to users' demands, biometric information, body temperature, sweat and internal pressures. Similarly, products can now become far more resilient and highly tuned to environmental changes including moisture content, temperature, pressure, altitude or sound. Unique and highly tuned products will be manufactured in completely new ways where materials are activated through ambient energies to come together on their own, reconfigure, mutate and replicate. Volume constraints in shipping will be dramatically reduced with flat-pack materials that are activated on delivery to full volume and functionality. Similarly, shipping materials themselves will have non-Newtonian-like properties and respond in custom ways to resist forces and reconfigure space-filling containers for auto-distributed loads.

All of these future programmable products will not just be thrown away when they fail; rather, they will error-correct and self-repair to meet new demands. And even when they become obsolete, they can self-disassemble for pure recyclability, breaking themselves down to their fundamental components to be reconstituted as new products with lifelike capabilities in the future.

4D Printing and programmable active materials thus offer exciting opportunities for the future of the products, and the shipping and manufacturing sectors. Transformative, multi-state, additive manufacturing will likely expand to become a palette of many materials with an almost limitless response to external forces. The Self-Assembly Lab aims to develop a full suite of 4D-Printed, fully customisable 'smart' materials that respond to various external energies with both single- and dual-phase transformations. ⌂

Notes

1. T Rowe Price, 'Infographic: A Brief History of 3D Printing', *Connections*, May 2012: http://individual.troweprice.com/public/Retail/Planning-&-Research/Connections/3D-Printing/Infographic.
2. David Chandler, 'Printing Off the Paper', *MIT News (Online)*, 2011: http://web.mit.edu/press/2011/3d-printing.html.
3. Michael Hayes, 'Developing and Deploying New Technologies – Industry Perspectives', Boeing presentation at the US Manufacturing Competitiveness Initiative Dialogue on Additive Manufacturing, Oak Ridge National Laboratory, Oak Ridge, Tennessee, 2013.
4. Skylar Tibbits, 'Design to Self-Assembly', in Achim Menges (ed), ⌂ *Material Computation: Higher Integration in Morphogenetic Design*, Vol 82, No 2, March/April, 2012, pp 68–73.
5. This work was developed at the Self-Assembly Lab, MIT, in collaboration with Shelly Linor, Daniel Dikovsky and Shai Hirsch at Stratasys and Carlos Olguin of Autodesk.

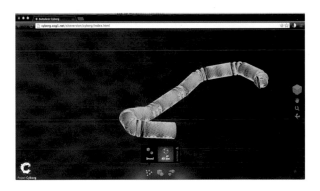

*Marta Malé-Alemany
and Jordi Portell*

SOFT TOLERANCE
AN APPROACH
FOR ADDITIVE
CONSTRUCTION
ON SITE

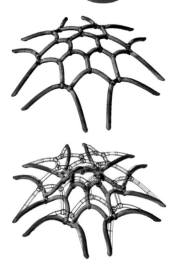

Does high precision have to result in highly defined slick forms? **Marta Malé-Alemany and Jordi Portell** of the FABbots research studio describe their unique approach that relies on the customisation of existing mechanical devices and the use of locally available materials. Though exacting in their execution of machine code, they maintain a delight in the natural characteristics of materials that are shaped with a 'soft tolerance'.

Miguel Guerrero, Chryssa Karakana, Carolina Miro and Anastasia Pistofidou, Areanna, FABbots 2.0, Institute for Advanced Architecture of Catalonia (IAAC), Barcelona, 2011
top: Binder flow simulation on a sand formation.
bottom: Structural deformation simulation of the hard network shell that results from removing the loose sand scaffold.

The majority of challenging architectural projects currently involve manufacturing precise building components with computer numerically controlled (CNC) industrial methods, as well as managing their accurate assembly during construction. The ongoing FABbots research agenda,[1] however, envisions an alternative approach using customised robotic tools for building on site with additive techniques, and exploring ideas of 3D printing matter in a continuum. It prioritises using locally available materials, re-engineering existing mechanical devices or making custom ones, and developing specialised software tools – simultaneously engaging material science, machine design and computation to guide the generation, simulation and evaluation of design solutions.

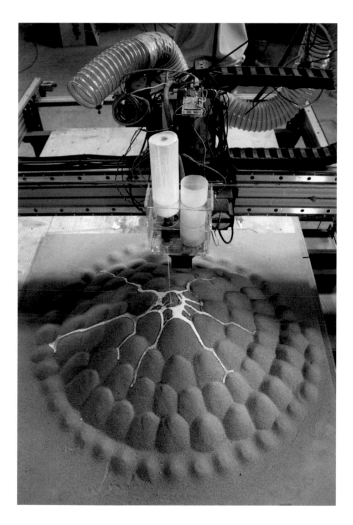

The resulting machine-material systems explore different ways to build an architecture that is only possible with additive tools, featuring complex material distributions that can integrate multifunctional performance. Design catalogues emerge through scripting the properties of the printed material, plausible machine printing trajectories and environmental data. Spatial opportunities arise naturally through thorough studies of the system – testing what is possible to build – revealing an intrinsic architectural language.

This approach thus relies on high precision in the generation and execution of the printing code, the operational capabilities of the machine, and the analysis of material properties and environmental physics. Yet the physical outcomes are often far from being slick or smoothly finished, as might be expected of high precision. What gets built does not follow a preconceived design and is not always predictable; it emerges from a beautiful tension between the strict execution of machine code and the more natural, textured or low-definition features of a material that is shaped within a soft tolerance, in real time and under varying conditions. Moreover, this relative inaccuracy is fully accepted, because it is the result of two fundamental choices: the use of abundant, natural construction materials (like clay or sand) which are heterogeneous and exhibit differential behaviour during deposition, solidification and/ or curing; and the hypothesis of deploying large-scale and customised fabrication devices on site, which implies that the printing process is also influenced by environmental changes.

Nasim Fashami, Saša Jokić and Starski Naya, FabClay,
FABbots 3.0, Institute for Advanced Architecture of
Catalonia (IAAC), Barcelona, 2012
Machine-material test running on a universal robot that has
been adapted with a customised end effector or nozzle
depositing clay.

Gabriel Bello, Alexandre Dubor, Akhil Kapadia and Angel Lara, Magnetic Architecture, FABbots 3.0, Institute for Advanced Architecture of Catalonia (IAAC), Barcelona, 2012
Complex formation of iron and binder matter, built by a robot that can position its forming magnetic clamp in multiple directions, challenging the effect of gravity.

These new computational tools facilitate generative design processes where material complexity, machine specifics and printing logics are the genesis of the design.

Single beam built with a magnetic clamp that allows the shaping of a mix of recycled iron and a polymeric binder under the effect of magnetic forces.

Considering these material dimensional changes or irregularities, as well as the effect of the context, the FABbots projects explore printing processes with continuous adaptation and feedback. In order to combine and employ these dynamics as a creative design source, custom software is developed from the ground up. Adaptability then lies in the printing code or program; in its capacity to handle flowing data, its robustness to evaluate the data and generate new machine instructions. These new computational tools facilitate generative design processes where material complexity, machine specifics and printing logics are the genesis of the design.

In opposition to the tendency found in industrial environments, which aims at achieving always smoother and finer results, FABbots promotes an additive fabrication approach that plays with built-in tolerances and welcomes the unpredictable beauty of emergent forms, valuing their material expression and texture. This is key to working with materials that are suitable for construction yet behave irregularly, and machines that can work autonomously on site but are exposed to unregulated conditions.

Large-scale additive fabrication thus begins by welcoming printing deviations and material flaws in a creative way, and follows by developing design catalogues that are conceived as printing code based on soft tolerance. As we move towards on-site deployment and implementation at 1:1, this approach seems a promising way to develop, adopt and seek applications for additive manufacturing methods in architecture. ᗪ

Note
1. FABbots is the agenda of a series of design and research studios directed by Marta Malé-Alemany at different schools of architecture. It includes a collection of 27 projects developed by Masters-level students working in teams. The studios were supported by expert tutors in computation and fabrication (Victor Viña, Cesar Cazares, Jeroen van Ameijde, Daniel Piker, Luis Fraguada, Brian Peters, Jordi Portell and Miquel Lloveras) and consultants in engineering (Santiago Martin Laguna and Santiago Martin González).

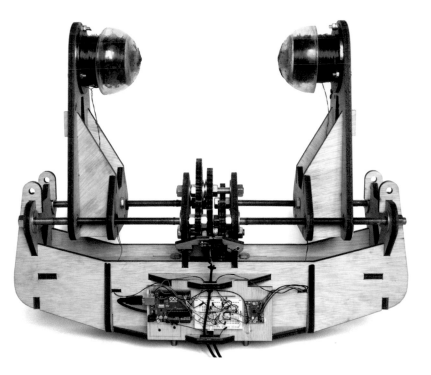

top: Magnetic clamp attached to an industrial milling machine ready to be tested in a three-axes environment.

above: Custom-made, digitally controlled magnetic clamp to be used as an end effector or forming nozzle on an industrial milling machine or universal robot.

WHY WE NEED ARCHITECTURE OF TOLERANCE

Professor and Chair in Integrated Design at the University of Calgary Faculty of Environmental Design, **Branko Kolarevic** has established an international reputation as an author and commentator on digital design and manufacturing in architecture. Here he questions the importance of high-definition tolerance in construction itself. As an industry that operates at far greater sizes and scales than other manufacturing bases, has the 'messy world of building' not always had to allow for a reasonable tolerance of errors? Should high-definition processes, which negate or negotiate zero tolerance, really be for architects and construction professionals the Holy Grail that they first appear?

Men were not intended to work with the accuracy of tools, to be precise and perfect in all their actions. If you will have that precision out of them, and make their fingers measure degrees like cog-wheels, and their arms strike curves like compasses, you must unhumanize them.
— John Ruskin, *The Stones of Venice*, 1853[1]

Over the past few weeks I have been watching the crews do their work on a construction site across the street where a 16-storey building is going up. Despite all the mighty machines they have at their disposal, and all the digital technologies now available to the building industry, a surprising amount of work is being done manually, more or less in the same way it was for much of the 20th century. The formwork for the casting of concrete is manually assembled, the steel rebars manually shaped, placed and tied in place, and the concrete poured and spread on horizontal surfaces and manually finished. One can only imagine the mistakes made (as evidenced by the sound of pneumatic drills the next day). When it started to rain, a small puddle of water on one of the large concrete

slabs that was poured and finished the day before grew bigger. I do not think that anyone needed a 3D laser scanner to realise that the slab was not flat; such relative inaccuracy in material production (discussed by Marta Malé-Alemany and Jordi Portell on pp 122–7 of this issue) is acceptable – and tolerated.

Apparently, all those errors – an inch or two here and an inch or two over there – do not matter much because the industry has its own standard margins of error, tolerances that are manageable given the sheer scale and size of the building and the manual labour deployed on the site. As long as things are 'more or less' there (as Enric Miralles would put it),[2] the building's concrete shell will continue to go up; precisely manufactured curtain-wall components will then be fitted to the building's shell, with some cleverly designed adjustable connections to compensate for any deviations of the constructed geometry from what was designed and laboriously defined in thick sets of construction drawings.

Construction in the 21st century: some high-tech, largely low-tech, and much manual labour.

Gramazio & Kohler, mTable customisable table series, 2002
Different mTables (with holes) designed by customers using an interactive, parametric app created by Fabio Gramazio and Matthias Kohler.

The building industry is tolerant of errors (within reason) and it knows how to deal with them. Its acceptable margins of error look huge compared to other production environments, but if one factors in the size and scale at which it operates, the differences in tolerances – relatively speaking – are not that great. For example, my iPhone was assembled probably with tolerances measured in hundredths of an inch; if I were to scale up the iPhone to a 16-storey tower, roughly by a factor of 400, that 0.005-inch tolerance (which I am guessing at) would be comparable to 2 inches on a 16-storey tower – which we would think of as being an Apple-like degree of precision.

So, what is the point that I am trying to make?

In my view, 'zero tolerance' is an oxymoron in the context of the building industry, and a goal that is probably not worth pursuing. There are certainly components, such as curtain walls, in which a much greater degree of precision is needed because water- and air-tightness are requirements that must be satisfied. Tight tolerances (which should not be mistaken for no- or zero tolerances) are also tied to the kinds of materials used in tectonic assemblies; some materials, such as metals and glass, can be CNC machined with considerable precision (as opposed to concrete casting).

Even if zero tolerances were to exist in the production and assembly of buildings, they would probably be counterproductive. Buildings operate in conditions with large temperature

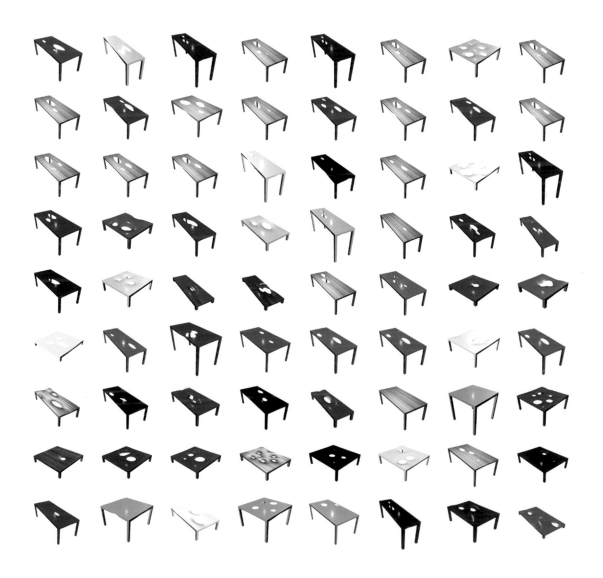

variations, to which different materials react differently. For example, a metal bar that connects two wooden parts can expand at a different rate to wood in hot weather, creating a gap where there was none when it was cold (say, during the night). In addition to the influence of differential temperatures, another important factor are the deflections under dead or live loads (or wind loads), which can contribute significantly to the dynamics of built assemblies. For example, deflection under load is often a significant issue in designing and constructing heavy cladding panels and masonry walls.

Such differential behaviour in varying environmental conditions has resulted in a rich tradition of tectonic ingenuity where material and load dynamics – and the dimensional variation that results from them – could be accommodated without any functional loss. As a consequence, good designers and engineers plan for precision and tolerance issues, allowing size variations and imperfections in interfaces between (nowadays digitally fabricated) components and the rest of the building by providing adjustment points – designed opportunities for on-site adjustment during assembly.

Tolerances Are Everywhere

Even if one were to focus on the world of production alone, one would discover a very rich language related to the margins of error (tolerances). A common definition of 'tolerance' is that it refers to a permissible limit (or limits) of variation in a physical dimension, or a measured value or physical property of a material, manufactured object or system. Dimensions or properties can vary within certain limits without affecting significantly the functioning of a product (or a process). Tolerances are specified to allow for imperfections and inherent variability without compromising performance. The building industry knows how to deal with imperfections (such as the slight sag in the poured concrete slab) and inherent variability (such as different

thermal behaviour) without compromising performance. Lawsuits emerge when that is not the case (as in the famous water leaks in Frank Gehry's Stata Center at Massachusetts Institute of Technology).[3]

It is well understood in any manufacturing context that the actual production of any product (or operation of any system) involves some inherent variation of input and output. Measurement error and statistical uncertainty are present in all measurements, including those done with 3D laser scanning. Dimensional tolerances in production are supplemented with the 'fit' in assemblies, which can be defined as a designed – that is, planned – clearance, interference or transition between two parts (and all are applicable to building assemblies). Within each of these categories of fit are several classes ranging from high precision and narrow tolerance to lower precision and wider tolerance. The choice of fit is determined first based on the use (function), and second by the manufacturability of the parts.

In manufacturing, allowances are distinct from tolerances. An allowance is a 'planned' (designed) deviation from an ideal, as opposed to tolerance, which is an expected but 'unplanned' deviation. The two terms are often interchanged because both refer to what is permissible, or what is acceptable. The world of mechanical engineering has a so-called geometric dimensioning and tolerancing (GD&T) system for defining and communicating engineering tolerances. This notation standard for engineering drawings and three-dimensional solid models describes explicitly nominal geometry and its allowable variation.

In manufacturing, tolerances are assigned to parts as boundaries for acceptable build. No CNC machine can hold dimensions

precisely to the nominal value, with zero tolerance, so there must be acceptable degrees of variation. Designing for variation – imperfections in production and assembly – is a historic necessity in the building industry that is unlikely to disappear any time soon.

Design Tolerances and Tolerance of Use

The Taguchi Loss Function, developed by the Japanese business statistician Genichi Taguchi to measure financial loss to society resulting from poor quality in production, shows how the quality is not significantly diminished if a designed tolerance is exceeded in production; a perceived loss progressively increases with the variation from the intended condition. When Taguchi's work became known to a wider audience courtesy of W Edwards Deming[4] (through his prominent role in the 'quality movement' in the US), it was considered a breakthrough in quality-control thinking, underlining the importance of designing for variation.

Another important tenet of Taguchi's quality philosophy is 'off-line quality control', the designing of products and processes so that they are not affected by the parameters that are outside of the designer's control. This is reminiscent of error-tolerant design, in which so-called 'forcing functions' or 'behaviour-shaping constraints' are used as techniques to prevent errors (known as *poka-yoke* in Japan, meaning mistake-proofing).

This raises the issue of design tolerance, which is much more interesting to contemplate than production or assembly tolerances. For example, in the mass customisation of products, in which customers choose essential dimensions and key features of products using an interactive system, designers of parametric systems (that define the

Tolerances are specified to allow for imperfections and inherent variability without compromising performance.

boundaries of the design space explored by customers) operate with dimensional ranges instead of discrete, fixed dimensions – they set out thresholds, upper and lower limits. A parametrically defined design space can result in thousands of different designs authored by the customers using an interactive, parametric system created by the designer. Obviously some of the generated designs could be barely functional or very ugly, which poses interesting design challenges of encoding only 'good' designs, and coding out 'bad' designs. Arguably, such design-wise 'quality control' might be possible in the functional realm, but aesthetics are a different matter altogether, which would require quantifying the qualitative (and highly subjective). In my view, such design environments demand a certain degree of design tolerance for customer-designed products that are aesthetically unacceptable to the designer, but with which the customer is pleased. Is there a point at which parametrically defined, interactively designed, digitally fabricated, mass-customised product is beyond control?

Finally, there is what one could refer to as the 'tolerance in use'. In 'Identity, Intimacy and Domicile: Notes on the Phenomenology of Home', Juhani Pallasmaa writes about the 'architecture of tolerance', the architect's margin of tolerance in facilitating the personalisation of space.[5] Pallasmaa makes a distinction between 'architecture of accommodation' and 'architecture of rejection', the latter not incorporating 'personal identity, memories and dreams of the inhabitant'. He then writes about and expresses his clear preference for architectural design that 'can allow and absorb aesthetic deviation without resulting in undesirable conflict' and mentions the architecture and furniture of Alvar Aalto as having 'great aesthetic tolerance'.

Precision Matters, But Absolute Precision is Inconsequential

As Ilona Gaynor and Benedict Singleton note in this issue, 'there is a certain pleasure to be found in a thing well made' (see pp 48–53). Precision does matter – that is patently obvious: 'without a certain minimum degree of precision, a building does not stand up,' as those authors state. But architecture of zero tolerance, of absolute precision, which it implies – whether in design, production or use – is a pursuit of questionable merits, unnecessary and unattainable. As Gaynor and Singleton point out, if the digital technologies of production and measurement, discussed in this issue, implicitly posit a principle of zero tolerance as a horizon that architecture can approach, then that invites an exploration of an aesthetic of precision as a quality of design in general (and not the precision afforded by a given system or technology). Such a pursuit, however, 'foregrounds the risk of precise architectural action – what is gambled in narrowing margins of space and time, where exactness matters and becomes a force in its own right'. Why would that be worth chasing? Towards what ends?

Imperfections and inherent variability – the 'errors' – are a fact of life in the messy world of building. They will never disappear from the act of designing and producing architecture. 'The principle of zero tolerance,' however, as noted by Gaynor and Singleton, 'is unforgiving of error.' They are absolutely right about that: zero tolerance does not belong in the vocabulary of architecture. ⌂

Notes
1. John Ruskin, 'The Nature of Gothic', in G Lees-Maffei and R Houze (eds), *The Design History Reader*, Berg Publishers (Oxford), 2010, p 62 (first published in 1853).
2. Enric Miralles, 'More or Less…', public lecture at the University of Hong Kong Faculty of Architecture, 17 January 1997.
3. Robin Pogrebin and Katie Zezima, 'MIT Sues Frank Gehry, Citing Flaws in Center He Designed', *New York Times*, 6 November 2007, p A19.
4. W Edwards Deming, *Out of the Crisis*, MIT Press (Cambridge, MA), 2000 (first published in 1982).
5. Juhani Pallasmaa, 'Identity, Intimacy and Domicile: Notes on the Phenomenology of Home', *Encounters: Architectural Essays*, Rakennustieto Oy (Helsinki), 2005, pp 111–26.

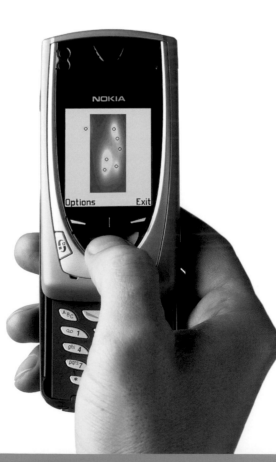

The mTable can be customised using a mobile phone app and then digitally fabricated.

Sarat Babu is a material scientist and designer. He is founder of Betatype, a material design and research firm focusing on developing advanced hybrid materials using additive manufacturing for future products. In addition, he is currently a musculoskeletal device designer in the Department of Surgery, Imperial College London, and a doctoral candidate on the EngD VEIV programme, University College London (UCL) via employee secondment. He holds degrees in materials science and engineering, industrial design engineering and virtual environments imaging and visualisation, and has an Industrial Fellowship from the Royal Commission of 1851.

Richard Beckett is a scientist and architect. He is a teaching fellow at the Digital Manufacturing Centre (DMC London), a 3D print bureau and research facility within the Bartlett School of Architecture, UCL. He is also a design tutor for the Bartlett's Unit 20 with Marcos Cruz and Marjan Colletti. With a background in biochemistry, his work explores his interest in the realm between science, materials and architecture through developing digital techniques and physical output.

Philip Beesley is a professor in the School of Architecture at the University of Waterloo where he also serves as Director for the Integrated Group for Visualization, Design and Manufacturing, and as Director for Riverside Architectural Press. His Toronto-based practice, Philip Beesley Architect, Inc (PBAI), is an interdisciplinary design firm that incorporates industrial design, digital prototyping and mechatronics engineering.

Ilona Gaynor is a filmmaker, designer, and co-founder of the design and research studio The Department of No. Her work has been exhibited internationally, and she regularly teaches at the Bartlett School of Architecture, UCL, the Architectural Association (AA) and Princeton. She was the recipient of the 2011 Ridley Scott Award.

Ruairi Glynn is a lecturer on interactive architecture at the Bartlett School of Architecture, UCL, directing studios in MArch Graduate Architectural Design and MSc Adaptive Architecture and Computing. He practises as an installation artist, with recent exhibitions at Tate Modern, London, the Centre Pompidou, Paris, and the National Art Museum of China in Beijing. He has co-edited two books on the driving influence of computation in design: *Fabricate: Making Digital Architecture* (Riverside Architectural Press, 2011) with Bob Sheil; and *Digital Architecture: Passages Through Hinterlands* (2009) with Sara Shafiei.

Andrew Hudson-Smith is Director and Deputy Chair of the Bartlett Centre for Advanced Spatial Analysis (CASA) at UCL. He is a Reader in Digital Urban Systems and a Fellow of the Royal Society of Arts. His work can be found online at www.digitalurban.org.

Birgir Örn Jónsson was born in Reykjavik. He studied at the Royal Danish Academy of Fine Arts in Copenhagen and at the Bartlett School of Architecture, UCL, where he was awarded an MArch in Architecture with distinction in 2012. He has worked as an architectural designer, maker and researcher on a wide range of projects in London, Copenhagen and Reykjavik, and is currently based in London.

Branko Kolarevic is a Professor and Chair in Integrated Design at the University of Calgary Faculty of Environmental Design. He has taught architecture at several universities in North America and Asia, and has lectured worldwide on the use of digital technologies in design and production. He has authored, edited or co-edited several books, including *Manufacturing Material Effects* (Routledge, 2008), *Performative Architecture* (Routledge, 2004) and *Architecture in the Digital Age* (Taylor & Francis, 2003). He holds doctoral and masters degrees in design from Harvard University and a diploma engineer in architecture degree from the University of Belgrade.

Brandon Kruysman is a design technologist at design and engineering studio Bot&Dolly, specialising in automation, robotics and filmmaking. He graduated from the Southern California Institute of Architecture (SCI-Arc) with a Masters in Architecture, and was thereafter appointed as the first SCI-Arc Robot House Fellow, a year-long teaching and research fellowship that focused exclusively on advanced multi-robot fabrication. During this time he was the lead developer in a designer-friendly animation-based platform for collaborative robotic motion control. He has previously worked in the offices of Point b Design and THEVERYMANY, focusing exclusively on computational design and coded assemblies.

Tim Lucas joined Price & Myers in 1996 after graduating from Leeds University. In 2001 he founded the firm's Geometrics group, which specialises in structurally and geometrically advanced projects. He became a partner of Price & Myers in 2007. He has been responsible for the structural design of a wide variety of buildings, bridges and large-scale sculptures in a diverse range of structural materials including stainless steel, stone, bronze, timber and Ductal. He is a technical tutor at the Bartlett School of Architecture, UCL.

Marta Malé-Alemany is an architect, researcher and educator from Barcelona. Since 1997 she has combined her professional practice with teaching experimental design studios and research seminars in architecture schools in both the US and Europe in combination with directing several Masters programmes in architecture. Her current research agenda (FABbots) focuses on developing innovative material and construction solutions using customised robotic devices. She holds a Masters degree in Advanced Architectural Design from Columbia University, New York, and is currently a PhD candidate at the Escola Tècnica Superior d'Arquitectura de Barcelona (ETSAB), investigating the potential of large-scale additive manufacturing technologies to innovate building construction.

Tobias Nolte is a designer based in Berlin and New York. He is currently Director at Gehry Technologies where he has been working with leading international design firms including Gehry Partners, Zaha Hadid Architects, Snøhetta, UNStudio, Coop Himmelb(l)au and several others. Prior to Gehry Technologies he was a research fellow at Harvard Graduate School of Design (GSD) and worked for Preston Scott Cohen, Inc. He has taught courses on digital design

at the École Spéciale d'Architecture in Paris and the University of Applied Arts Vienna. He studied in Berlin and Los Angeles and holds an engineering diploma in architecture from the Technische Universität Berlin.

John Palmesino is an architect and urbanist. With Ann-Sofi Rönnskog he established Territorial Agency, an independent organisation that combines architecture, analysis, advocacy and action for integrated spatial transformation of contemporary territories. He is currently convening Diploma Unit 4 at the Architectural Association (AA) in London, where he has also initiated The AA Think Tank on territorial transformations. He is researching for his PhD at the Research Architecture Centre at Goldsmiths, University of London, where he also teaches the MA. He has been a research advisor at the Jan van Eyck Academie, Maastricht, and previously led the research activities of ETH Zurich/Studio Basel. He is a founding member of Multiplicity. Projects include the Anthropocene Observatory, Museum of Infrastructural Unconscious, North, Unfinishable Markermeer, USE Uncertain States of Europe, Mutations and Solid Sea.

Ralph Parker is a practising architect with more than 13 years' experience of architectural design and construction in the UK, New Zealand and China. Between 2000 and 2004 he worked for Marks Barfield Architects, during which time he designed and built the Spiral Café in Birmingham, which won an RIBA award, and was long-listed for the Stirling Prize. He is a founding partner of Honey, an art and architecture practice based in London. Since 2006 he has worked part time in Price & Myers' Geometrics group,

specialising in the design and construction of complex structures, alongside several notable artists and architects including Richard Wilson, Shirazeh Houshiary, Heather Ackroyd and Dan Harvey, and Martin Richman.

Jordi Portell is a practising registered architect who has become increasingly dedicated to research as a result of being a Masters-level student, and later an assistant faculty, of the FABbots research studio directed by Marta Malé-Alemany. He holds a professional degree in architecture from ETSAB, Barcelona, and a Masters in Advanced Architecture from the Institute for Advanced Architecture of Catalonia. His research is focused on the application of additive manufacturing techniques in architecture, with special interest in multi-material systems and complex material networks.

Jonathan Proto is a design technologist at design and engineering studio Bot&Dolly, specialising in automation, robotics and filmmaking. He graduated from SCI-Arc with a Masters in Architecture, and was thereafter appointed as the first SCI-Arc Robot House Fellow, a year-long teaching and research fellowship that focused exclusively on advanced multi-robot fabrication. During this time he was the lead developer of custom machine tooling through a variety of digital and analogue methods of making. He has honed his craft while working in the offices of Point b Design and THEVERYMANY, where he oversaw the execution of complex building components from conception through installation.

Ann-Sofi Rönnskog is an architect and urbanist. With John Palmesino she established Territorial Agency, an independent organisation that combines architecture, analysis, advocacy and action for integrated spatial transformation of contemporary territories. She is currently convening Diploma Unit 4 at the Architectural Association (AA) in London, where she has initiated The AA Think Tank on territorial transformations. She is a research fellow at the Oslo School of Architecture and Design (AHO) and at the Centre for Research Architecture, Goldsmiths, University of London. She was previously a researcher at ETH Zurich/Studio Basel. Recent projects include the Anthropocene Observatory, Museum of Infrastructural Unconscious, North and Unfinishable Markermeer.

Matthew Shaw is a designer, maker and educator based in London. His work is driven by the speculative use of digital technologies, the impact these technologies will have on our lives and the way they shape our architecture. He is co-founder of ScanLAB Projects, a tutor at the Bartlett School of Architecture, UCL, and director of Graticule Architecture.

Benedict Singleton is a designer and writer who lives and works in London, where he co-founded and directs, with Ilona Gaynor, the design and research studio The Department of No. He writes widely on design, philosophy, and the history and future of technology for publications including *Δ*, *e-flux* and *Collapse*.

Skylar Tibbits is Director of the Self-Assembly Lab at the Massachusetts Institute of Technology (MIT). He is a trained architect, designer and computer scientist whose research focuses on self-assembly and programmable material technologies. He is currently a faculty member in MIT's Department of Architecture, teaching graduate and undergraduate design studios and co-teaching the 'How to Make (Almost) Anything' seminar at MIT's Media Lab. He was recently awarded a 2013 Architectural League Prize and a TED Senior Fellowship, and was named a 'Revolutionary Mind' in *SEED Magazine's* 2008 design issue. He has a Bachelor of Architecture from Philadelphia University, as well as a Master of Science in Design and Computation and a Master of Science in Computer Science from MIT.

William Trossell graduated from the Bartlett School of Architecture, UCL, in 2009. Since completing his Masters in Architecture he has created structures, sculptures and events that draw on an extensive understanding of digital fabrication. He is co-founder of ScanLAB Projects and a tutor at the Bartlett.

Michael Webb studied architecture at the then Regent Street Polytechnic School of Architecture (now the University of Westminster) from 1953 to 1972. A project he designed during his fourth year was featured in the 'Visionary Architecture' exhibition at the Museum of Modern Art (MoMA), New York, in 1961. His thesis project for an entertainments centre in the middle of London was widely published, and was featured in the 'First Projects' exhibition at the Architectural Association (AA), London, in November 2009. In 1963, he was invited by Peter Cook to be part of an assortment of young architects who referred to themselves as the Archigram group, after the name of the magazine they started publishing, who rebelled against what they saw as the failure of the architectural establishment in Britain to produce buildings reflecting the dynamic changes, both technological and social, the country was then undergoing. For the last 17 years a large exhibition of the group's work has been touring world capitals; and in 2006 the group was awarded the Gold Medal from the Royal Institute of British Architects (RIBA). He sees his *raison d'être* as deriving from the drawings he has produced over the years, including those for the *Temple Island Study*, which resulted in an eponymous book published by the AA in 1987, and the *Drive-in House* series. He has had one-man shows at the Cooper Union where he now teaches, at Columbia University, the Storefront Gallery, Architecture League and the University of Buffalo in New York, the University of Manitoba at Winnipeg and the Art Net Gallery in London. He was a fellow at the Canadian Centre for Architecture (CCA) in Montreal from 2010 to 2011.

Andrew Witt is a designer who is trained as both an architect and mathematician. He is Research Advisor at Gehry Technologies (GT), and a lecturer in architecture at Harvard University. He was previously a director at GT's Paris office, where he consulted on geometry and technology for clients including Gehry Partners, Ateliers Jean Nouvel, UNStudio and Coop Himmelb(l)au. He has lectured widely including at the Bartlett School of Architecture, UCL, Princeton, MIT, Yale, Stanford and Vienna. He received an MArch (with distinction, AIA medal) and an MDes (with distinction) from Harvard.

INDIVIDUAL BACKLIST ISSUES OF *AD* ARE AVAILABLE FOR PURCHASE AT £24.99 / US$45

TO ORDER AND SUBSCRIBE SEE BELOW

What is *Architectural Design*?

Founded in 1930, *Architectural Design* (*AD*) is an influential and prestigious publication. It combines the currency and topicality of a newsstand journal with the rigour and production qualities of a book. With an almost unrivalled reputation worldwide, it is consistently at the forefront of cultural thought and design.

Each title of *AD* is edited by an invited guest-editor, who is an international expert in the field. Renowned for being at the leading edge of design and new technologies, *AD* also covers themes as diverse as architectural history, the environment, interior design, landscape architecture and urban design.

Provocative and inspirational, *AD* inspires theoretical, creative and technological advances. It questions the outcome of technical innovations as well as the far-reaching social, cultural and environmental challenges that present themselves today.

For further information on *AD*, subscriptions and purchasing single issues see: www.architectural-design-magazine.com

How to Subscribe

With 6 issues a year, you can subscribe to *AD* (either print, online or through the *AD* App for iPad).

INSTITUTIONAL SUBSCRIPTION
£212/US$398 print or online

INSTITUTIONAL SUBSCRIPTION
£244/US$457 combined print & online

PERSONAL-RATE SUBSCRIPTION
£120/US$189 print and iPad access

STUDENT-RATE SUBSCRIPTION
£75/US$117 print only

To subscribe to print or online:
Tel: +44 (0) 1243 843 272
Email: cs-journals@wiley.com

AD APP FOR iPAD
For information on the *AD* App for iPad go to www.architectural-design-magazine.com
6-issue subscription: £44.99/US$64.99
Individual issue: £9.99/US$13.99

THE INNOVATION IMPERATIVE
ARCHITECTURES OF VITALITY

Volume 83 No 1
ISBN 978 1119 978657

COMPUTATION WORKS
THE BUILDING OF ALGORITHMIC THOUGHT

Volume 83 No 2
ISBN 978 1119 952862

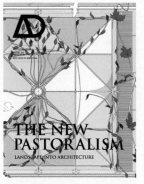

THE NEW PASTORALISM
LANDSCAPE INTO ARCHITECTURE

Volume 83 No 3
ISBN 978 1118 336984

SYSTEM CITY.
INFRASTRUCTURE AND THE SPACE OF FLOWS

Volume 83 No 4
ISBN 978 1118 361429

DRAWING ARCHITECTURE

Volume 83 No 5
ISBN 978 1118 418796

THE ARCHITECTURE OF TRANSGRESSION

Volume 83 No 6
ISBN 978 1118 361795

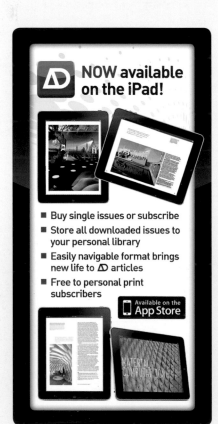